Gastric Sleeve Bariatric Co

2000 Days Of Tasty Recipes For Healthy Stomach Recovery And Quick Weight Loss After Surgery. Bonus: Conscious Eating Tips for Long-Term Results 28-Week Meal Plan

Raven Foster

Scan The QR Code
To Download Your Bonuses:

- 1-Year Gastric Sleeve Journal
- The Bariatric Meal Prep Masterclass

Contents

Introduction

Welcome to the Gastric Sleeve Gastric Cookbook!

This book is meant to accompany you on your journey to a healthier weight after gastric sleeve surgery.
We understand that undergoing gastric sleeve surgery and starting a new diet can be overwhelming,
We would like you to know that you do not stand alone in this.

This cookbook provides delicious and nutritious recipes to help make your transition to a healthier lifestyle more accessible.
In this cookbook, you will find 2000 days of delicious recipes tailored to the four gastric sleeve diet plan phases:
Clear liquid, Full liquid, Semi-solid, and Solid phase.

We've also included an 8-week meal plan divided into four diet phases to help you stay on track, useful guidelines for each stage, the best tips for long-term weight loss goals after surgery, and a complete list of foods to eat and avoid for each phase.

In addition, we have included a Bonus chapter on mindful eating, tips for dining out and navigating social situations while on a diet, and a 20-week meal plan for the maintenance phase.

We believe nourishing your body with healthy food, and your mind with positive thoughts and habits is essential.
We are excited to be a part of your journey to lose weight, and we hope that this cookbook will help you reach your goal.

Chapter 1: The Diet

1.1 Goals of the diet

- **Aid in healing:** The diet is designed to provide the patient with the necessary nutrients to help the stomach and body heal properly after the surgery.
- **Promote weight loss:** The diet is designed to be low in calories and high in protein to promote weight loss.
- **Reduce hunger and cravings:** The diet is designed to help the patient feel full faster and for more extended periods, which can reduce appetite and cravings.
- **Promote nutrient absorption:** The diet is designed to provide the patient with the necessary vitamins and minerals to help ensure proper nutrient absorption.
- **Help form new eating habits:** Following a strict diet after surgery encourages patients to develop new, healthy eating habits that will help them maintain their weight loss long-term.
- **Prepare for solid foods**: The patient will gradually progress through the different stages of the diet to prepare the stomach and digestive system for solid food.

1.2 The four phases

1. **Clear liquid phase:** This phase usually starts immediately after surgery and lasts for about 1-2 days. The patient can only consume clear liquids such as water, broth, clear juice, and plain tea or coffee.

2. **Full liquid phase**: This phase usually lasts for about 2-3 weeks, during which the patient can consume full liquids such as milk, cream, smoothies, and protein shakes.

3. **Semi-solid phase:** This phase usually lasts for about 2-3 weeks, during which the patient can consume pureed or mashed foods such as cooked vegetables, fruits, and protein sources.

4. **Solid phase:** This phase usually lasts for about 2-3 weeks, during which the patient can consume solid foods, but they must be cut into small, bite-size pieces and chewed thoroughly.

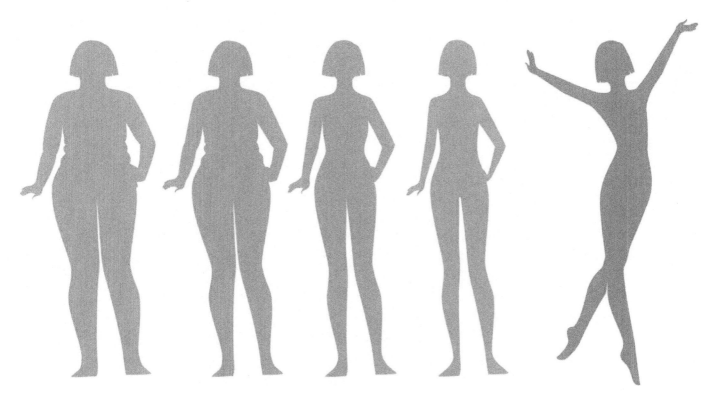

1.3 Recommendations for All Stages

It's time to begin preparing for your recovery, whether you are considering having bariatric surgery or have already set a date for the operation. Bariatric surgery would be a transformative treatment for individuals who need to shed much weight. The most significant adjustment you'll need to make in your diet. Following your bariatric procedure, we've described 4 stages of eating that you might anticipate:

First Stage: Clear Liquids

You will begin a clear liquid regimen the day following your operation and follow it for around 4–5 days. Try your hardest to gradually increase the number of clear liquids you consume daily during this period to roughly 3 oz every 30 minutes. After your treatment, this could be challenging, but it will gradually get better, and you will feel more at ease. Drink gently at this time and avoid using a straw or chewing gum, which can cause bloating and gas. Here are some samples of drinks to test out:

- Diluted apple juice
- Pedialyte popsicles
- Lemon water
- Citrus gelatin (sugar-free)

- Vegetable broth
- Lemon-Lime Gatorade G2

- Protein smoothies that have been diluted should also be a part of your diet. Use ½ protein shake and ½ glass of water

Second Stage: Full Liquids

After 4–5 days and when you can manage 48 oz of clear liquids daily, you can go on to phase 2 of this diet. This phase lasts roughly 7–10 days and features mushy meals and consistency like yogurt. Attempt to eat every 3–4 hours, being careful not to miss any meals. Each dish's serving size should be around 1/2 cup or 2 oz. You should continue consuming fluids in at least 48–64 oz throughout this period. You could eat a variety of meals during this phase, for instance:

- Greek/non-dairy yogurt
- Cottage cheese
- Oatmeal/Cream of Wheat
- Mashed banana

- Unsweetened applesauce
- Mushroom soup cream, pea soup, etc.
- Black beans, fat-free beans, or lentils (blended)

With a target of 80–100 g of protein per day, you should continue consuming protein between meals. Start blending protein with unsweetened soy or almond milk; avoid cow's milk. On the fifth day of this stage, you should also start taking vitamins and minerals, adding one more each day.

Third Stage: Soft and Moist Foods

The third phase of your diet would start around 2 weeks after your procedure and last 2 complete weeks. Each meal would be around 1/2 cup and 4 oz in size and be simple to take apart with a fork. Even if you haven't consumed this quantity, you must stop eating as quickly as you feel full! In this period, soft meals like the following can be consumed:

- Lean proteins, such as slow-cooked chicken/pork
- Canned chicken/tuna/crab
- Over-cooked vegetables, including zucchini, cauliflower, squash, or mushrooms
- Egg whites

- Soft cheeses (low-fat)
- Chili or stew
- Refried beans, chickpeas, mashed lentils, and tofu
- Salmon, trout, or flakey fish
- Soft fruits, including peaches, melons, and avocados

Drink fluids as usual between meals, but remember the 30/30 rule: Avoid drinking anything for 30 minutes before or after your meal. Continually consume a protein beverage and minerals.

Fourth Stage: Regular Consistency

This stage comprises resuming regular foods and begins 4–6 weeks following your treatment. Start by introducing just 1–2 new items each day, and stay away from foods that make you bloated, such as broccoli, pepper, onions, and spicy dishes. Do not forget to chew your meal thoroughly before swallowing. No meal should be larger than 1 cup, or roughly 3/4 cup (6 oz). The 30/30 guideline should still be followed, and you should drink water between meals. You can eventually work your way up to a usual diet, but there are still several items you ought to stay away from:

- Rice, pasta, and bread
- Oils
- Alcohol

- Baked goods
- Carbonated drinks
- Added sugars

- Dry meats
- Fried foods
- Fruit with thick skin

1.4 Useful Tips For Each phase Of The Diet

Clear liquid phase:

- Drink at least 64 ounces of liquids per day to prevent dehydration
- Avoid carbonated and caffeinated beverages as they can cause discomfort
- Avoid red and purple liquids as they can be difficult to distinguish from blood
- Start with clear broths, then progress to clear juices, and then plain water
- Avoid sugar and artificial sweeteners

Full liquid phase:

- Continue to drink at least 64 ounces of liquids per day
- Include protein shakes or supplement drinks to ensure adequate protein intake
- Avoid carbonated and caffeinated beverages
- Gradually add cream or milk to your liquids
- Begin to introduce thicker liquids like yogurt and pudding.

Semi-solid phase:

- Continue to drink at least 64 ounces of liquids per day
- Add pureed or mashed fruits and vegetables to your diet
- Gradually introduce soft, easy-to-chew foods, such as eggs, fish, and well-cooked meat
- Avoid tough, fibrous foods, such as raw vegetables, nuts, and seeds
- Start taking vitamin and mineral supplements as advised by your dietician or surgeon

Solid phase:

- Continue to drink at least 64 ounces of liquids per day
- Gradually introduce solid foods, starting with small, bite-size pieces that are easy to chew
- Chew your food thoroughly to prevent discomfort and promote weight loss
- Avoid high-fat, high-sugar foods, such as fried foods and sweets
- Gradually increase portion size and frequency of meals as advised by your surgeon or dietician
- Continue taking vitamin and mineral supplements as advised by your dietician or surgeon
- It is essential to be patient with the process, as the body needs time to adjust to the new changes.

1.5 Foods to eat and to avoid for each phase

Clear liquid phase:

Foods to eat:

- Clear broths such as chicken, beef, or vegetable
- Clear juices such as apple or cranberry
- Water
- Ice chips
- Sugar-free Jell-O or popsicles
- Plain tea or coffee

Foods to avoid:

- Solid foods
- Milk or cream
- Carbonated drinks
- Juice with pulp
- Red or purple liquids
- Caffeinated drinks
- Alcohol

Full liquid phase:

Foods to eat:

- Protein shakes or supplement drinks
- Milk or cream
- Strained soups or broths
- Smoothies
- Yogurt
- Pudding
- Sugar-free Jell-O

Foods to avoid:

- Solid foods
- Carbonated drinks
- Caffeinated drinks
- Alcohol
- Juices with pulp
- Nuts and seeds

Semi-solid phase:

Foods to eat:

- Pureed or mashed fruits and vegetables
- Soft, easy-to-chew foods such as eggs, fish, and well-cooked meat
- Low-fat, low-sugar protein options such as chicken, turkey, fish, and tofu
- Cooked cereals
- Cooked beans
- Cooked rice
- Cooked pasta

Foods to avoid:

- Raw vegetables and fruits
- Tough, fibrous foods such as nuts and seeds
- Fried foods
- Sweets
- High-fat meats
- High-sugar foods

Solid phase:

Foods to eat:

- Small, bite-size pieces of cooked meats, fish, and poultry
- Cooked or steamed vegetables
- Cooked grains such as rice, pasta, or quinoa
- Cooked beans
- Low-fat dairy products
- Fruits

Foods to avoid:

- Fried foods
- Sweets
- High-fat meats
- High-sugar foods
- Tough, fibrous foods such as nuts and seeds
- Foods with added sugar or syrups
- Carbonated drinks
- Caffeinated drinks
- Alcohol

1.6 Top Tips for long-term weigh loss goals after surgery

Follow the recommended diet and exercise plan: Sticking to the diet and exercise plan recommended by your surgeon and dietician to achieve and maintain long-term weight loss is essential.

Keep track of your progress: Keep track of your weight loss progress, measurements, and how you feel; this will help you stay motivated and make any necessary adjustments to your diet and exercise plan.

Consistency is key: Maintaining a consistent lifestyle change is essential to achieve and maintain long-term weight loss. Consistency in eating habits and exercise will help you to achieve and maintain a healthy weight.

Eat a balanced diet: A balanced diet that includes protein, healthy fats, and complex Carbs is essential for weight loss and maintaining a healthy weight.

Stay hydrated: Drinking enough water will help you feel full and hydrated and aid digestion. Aim for at least 64 ounces of water per day.

Get enough sleep: Sleep is crucial to weight loss and overall health. Adequate sleep can help control hunger and improve overall energy levels.

Stay active: Regular physical activity is essential for weight loss and overall health. Aim for at least 30 minutes of moderate-intensity exercise per day.

Seek support: Surround yourself with a support system of friends, family, or a support group. They can help you stay motivated and on track with your weight loss goals.

Please don't be too hard on yourself: Remember that weight loss is a journey, and it's essential to be patient with yourself. Don't get discouraged if you have setbacks or slip-ups. Keep pushing forward and stay focused on your goals.

Keep in touch with your surgeon and dietician: Regular check-ins with your surgeon and dietician will help ensure that you are on track with your weight loss goals and making progress healthily.

A pouch reset serves as a post-op diet. The pouch reset routine is different because it is carried out over 5 days to get you back to eating smaller quantities. The pouch reset strategy might help former bariatric patients get back on track and lose weight.
Following it, you could either continue eating according to the pouch reset diet or return to the post-op routine that worked best for you.

2.1 To Whom Does a Pouch Reset Serve?

At some time in their life, everyone gains weight. There may be occasions when you cannot follow the post-operative diet since nobody is perfect. It's crucial to swiftly recuperate and modify your eating habits. Don't let a few indulgences spoil your progress since gaining weight is easier than losing it. If you haven't been on the right track with healthy eating habits for a while, this pouch reset plan could be an effective tool to get your stomach back to a more desirable size.

If you're searching for an intelligent food method, the pouch reset routine is for you. Also, this strategy is for you if:

- You've come to a stop or place you can no longer go.
- You've gained a little weight.
- Your total food intake exceeds 6 oz.
- You stopped recording your food intake.
- You desire to take back control of your eating patterns.
- You're worried that your sleeve or pouch has "stretched."

2.1 5-Day Gastric Sleeve Pouch Reset

First Day: Clear Liquids

Starting with the most challenging stage, a pouch reset plan moves on to solid meals. You're free to drink as many sugar-free liquids as you'd like, but if you want an extra energy boost, consider adding some nutrient-dense clean broths to your diet. Clear beverages will help your body become clean on Day 1 and agitate the ghrelin and leptin hormones, which control your hunger and sense of fullness.

- Water
- Sugar-free drinks (Crystal Light, Vitamin Zero Water, Mio, Powerade Zero, Propel, etc.)
- Broth (chicken, beef, or vegetable)
- Unsweetened tea
- Tea

Second Day: Thick Liquids

It's awesome that you've already reached Day 2 of the pouch reset diet. Protein in the form of thick liquids may be obtained from here. Protein shakes are the most effective way to consume whole liquids since blending them destroys all the nutrients from fruits and vegetables. Protein powders are the most practical way to include protein in a drink or smoothie. You should space out your 3 protein shakes every 2–3 hours.

- 3 protein shakes are to be consumed.
- 64 oz sugar-free beverages
- Weight Loss Magic Soup

Third-Day: Soft Solids

- 3 protein shakes
- Unlimited Weight Loss Magic Soup

You can choose 2 servings from the following selections of soft solid proteins:

- ½ cup cottage cheese
- ½ cup beans (whole or refried)
- 4 oz of tofu
- 2 poached/scrambled eggs
- 6 oz Greek yogurt

Fourth Day: Firm Solids

- 3 protein shakes
- Unlimited Weight Loss Magic Soup

Pick 2 servings from these daily protein intake foods:

- 4 oz chicken
- 4 oz fish
- 2 eggs
- 4 oz tofu

Pick 2 servings of fat every day:

- 15 almonds
- 1 tbsp oil, peanut butter, or butter
- ½ avocado

Fifth Day: Whole Foods

The same rules as Day 4 apply: leaner proteins can be used (including pork, venison, beef, etc.). Include 2 of your preferred Portions:

- ¼ cup beans
- ¼ cup sweet potato
- ¼ cup quinoa
- ¼ cup vegetables
- ¼ cup berries

Weight Loss Magic Soup

Total time: 30 minutes
Time for prep.: 10 minutes

Time for cook: 20 minutes
Portions: 2

Ingredients:

- 1 tablespoon of olive oil
- 1 minced onion
- 2 cloves of garlic, finely chopped
- 1 large, diced carrot
- 1 celery stalk diced and set aside.
- 1 can of tomatoes in diced
- 2 cups of broth made from vegetables
- 1 teaspoon of dried basil
- 1 teaspoon of oregano that has been dried
- 1/2 cup of sliced mushrooms,
- 1 pound green beans
- 1/2 cup zucchini, diced
- 1/2 cup of cooked brown rice
- Salt and pepper can be added to taste

Instructions:

1. Warm the olive oil in a large pot over medium heat.
2. in a bowl, Mix vegetable broth, diced tomatoes, basil, oregano, salt, and pepper
3. Cook for 5 minutes till the vegetables are soft.
4. In a mixing bowl, blend the vegetable broth, diced tomatoes, basil, oregano, salt, and pepper.
5. Bring the water to a boil.
6. Add cooked rice, green beans, zucchini, and mushrooms.
7. Cook for about 14 - 15 minutes until the vegetables are tender.
8. If desired, garnish with fresh herbs and serve hot.

Nutrition (per serving):

- Cal: 208
- Protein: 7g
- Carbs: 37g
- Fat: 6g
- Fiber: 6g
- Sodium: 793mg
- Sugar: 9g
- Cholesterol: 0mg

2.2 Guidelines for Pre and Post-Operation

Guidelines for Pre-Op Nutrition

Before surgery, you should eat as many nutrients as possible to fill your nutritional "bank account." Here are some tips for you to follow:

- **Consume adequate protein.** Be careful to get in at least 1–2 weeks of daily protein consumption before surgery. Your daily protein needs will depend on how much muscle you have, but studies have found that 65–100 g constitute the sweet spot. Our immune system, bones, and muscles are all built from protein. Before surgery, you must be as healthy as possible.
- **Purchase plenty of fruits and veggies.** Most snacks and meals include vegetables and fruits. Greens, particularly. Due to their high vitamin and mineral content—particularly the vitamins K, C, and magnesium—greens are fantastic for your skin and help heal muscles, cartilage, and bones.
- **Consume whole grains.** Include enough whole grains in your diet to give your body the B vitamins required to deal with stress.
- **Consume less of these.** Consider cutting out or limiting the amount of added caffeine, sugars, and alcohol in your diet. These put the body under additional stress and deprive it of nutrients that it needs to digest properly.

Guidelines for Post-Op Nutrition

Post-op dietary objectives enable quicker recovery and assist you in getting back to your favorite activities as soon as feasible. It's crucial to keep up a healthy diet after surgery.

- **Eat more often and in smaller portions if you've lost your appetite.** Some people experience appetite loss following surgery and when taking painkillers. However, surgery raises the body's calorie requirements, and <u>healing</u> requires extra Cal.
- **Include fiber.** Fiber supports regular bowel motions. Utilize fruits, veggies, cooked beans, or whole grains to add fiber to each snack and meal.
- **Consume adequate protein.** Muscles and bones benefit from eating protein at every meal. In addition to cooked dry beans, protein may be found in meat, soy, fish, dairy, eggs, nuts, and poultry.
- **A crucial component of bone is calcium.** Your doctor may advise calcium and vitamin D supplements if you don't receive enough calcium from your meals. Eat yogurt or cheese, and drink milk and calcium-fortified drinks.
- **The body uses vitamin C to create bones and repair wounds.** Citrus fruits, potatoes, green or red peppers, tomatoes, collard greens, strawberries, broccoli, and spinach all are sources of vitamin C.
- **Don't forget to drink lots of water.** Drink at least 6–8 cups of liquids daily to prevent constipation.

2.3 Importance of Physical Activity

One of the strategies for achieving and preserving your optimal health following surgery is exercise. Being active helps to:

- Keep your muscular mass and strength lean.
- Improve your bones' strength and joint stability.
- Boost your skin's suppleness following bariatric surgery.
- Keep losing weight after surgery.

Many patients who have had bariatric surgery also suffer from other health problems, like high blood pressure or diabetes, and find that regular exercise is essential to managing these disorders.

2.4 Food List

You should generally pick meals that are moderate to high in beneficial fats, low to moderate in carbs, and high to moderate in protein.

Good (healthy) fat-containing foods include:

- Avocados
- Coconut oil
- Salmon
- Nut butter
- Nuts

Next are some principles you should follow to stay healthy:

- Choose lean meats.
- Introduce new foods slowly.
- Consume canned salmon and tuna.
- Give food and water at least 30 minutes apart.
- Avoid greasy and spicy foods.
- Take high-quality nutritional supplements and vitamins.
- Avoid whole milk.
- Plan your meals.
- Eliminate fast food.
- Limit/eliminate desserts.
- Buy nutritious food.
- Eat nutrient-rich foods (whole meats, fruits, eggs, and vegetables)

3.1 Chicken Backs Broth

Time for cook: 4-5 hours, **Complexity level:** easy, **Time for prep.:** 10 minutes, **Portions:** 6

Ingredients

- 2 tbsp. of apple cider
- Water, as needed
- 4 chicken backs
- 2 carrots chopped
- 2 celery stalks chopped

Directions

1. In a pot, add chicken & enough water to cover.
2. Place on high flame & boil; turn the heat low & simmer.
3. Add vinegar & vegetables, cook for 4-5 hours, and keep adding water if it is low.
4. As it is cooked enough. Strain & serve.

Nutritional information

Carbs: 1 g, Cal: 50 kcal, Prt: 6 g, Fats: 8 g

3.2 Lemon Thyme Iced Tea

Time for cook: 15 minutes, **Complexity level:** easy, **Time for prep.:** 10 minutes, **Portions:** 3

Ingredients

- Lemons, one & a half
- Water, 4 cups
- Cinnamon Stick, 1 stick
- Black Tea, 2 bags, Decaffeinated
- Thyme, 1 tsp.

Directions

1. In a pot, add water & add all the ingredients except for tea bags.
2. Cook for a few minutes. Add tea bags. Turn the heat off.
3. Steep for 15 minutes, strain & serve.

Nutritional information

Carbs: 1 g, Cal: 30 kcal, Prt: 1 g, Fats: 1 g

3.3 Celery Juice

Time for cook: 15 minutes, **Complexity level:** easy, **Time for prep.:** 10 minutes, **Portions:** 1-2

Ingredients

- Ice, as needed
- 2-4 bunches of celery
- 1 cup of water

Directions

1. Add all ingredients to a blender.
2. Pulse until smooth, strain & serve.

Nutritional information

Carbs: 1 g, Cal: 10 kcal, Prt: 1 g, Fats: 0 g

3.4 Basic Vegetable Stock

Time for cook: 15 minutes, **Complexity level:** easy, **Time for prep.:** 10 minutes, **Portions:** 1-2

Ingredients

- 2 tbsp. of diced celery
- 1/4 cup of diced onions
- 1/4 cup of chopped cabbage
- 1/4 cup of cauliflower florets
- 1/4 cup of diced carrot

Directions

1. In a pot, add 3-4 cups of water.
2. Add all the vegetables. Boil on high flame for 10-20 minutes.
3. Strain & serve.

Nutritional information

Carbs: 1 g, Cal: 9 kcal, Prt: 1 g, Fats: 0 g

3.5 Clear Tomato Soup

Time for cook: 25 minutes, **Complexity level:** easy, **Time for prep.:** 10 minutes, **Portions:** 2

Ingredients

- 1 cup of diced onion
- 1 bay leaf
- 2 cups of chopped tomato
- 1 garlic clove
- 8 mint leaves
- Half tsp. of salt
- 3 cups of water
- Half tsp. of butter

Instructions

1. Add water, onion, garlic & tomato to a pan.
2. Cook on medium flame till tomatoes become tender.
3. With a stick blender, pulse until smooth.
4. Add butter to a pan with mint leaves & the bay leaf. Cook for a few minutes.
5. Add the tomato soup & salt, and cook for 5 minutes.
6. Strain & serve.

Nutritional information

Carbs: 4 g, Cal: 20 kcal, Prt: 5 g, Fats: 2 g

3.6 Warm Honey Green Tea

Time for cook: 10 minutes, **Complexity level:** easy, **Time for prep.:** 10 minutes, **Portions:** 4

Ingredients

- 4 lemon peel strips
- 4 slices of lemon
- 4 orange peel strips
- 4 cups of water
- 4 green tea bags
- 2 tsp. of honey

Instructions

1. In a pan, add orange & lemon peel with water.
2. Let it boil, turn the heat low & simmer for 10 minutes.
3. Strain & add honey to tea bags.
4. Steep for a few minutes, take the tea bags out & serve.

Nutritional information

Carbs: 5 g, Cal: 16 kcal, Prt: 1 g, Fats: 0 g

3.7 Lemon Basil Iced Tea

Time for cook: 15 minutes, **Complexity level:** easy, **Time for prep.:** 10 minutes, **Portions:** 2

Ingredients

- 6 fresh basil leaves
- 2 green tea bags
- Half lemon, sliced thin
- 3 cups of hot water

Directions

- In a jug, add all ingredients & steep.
- Strain & serve chilled.

Nutritional information

Carbs: 0 g, Cal: 8 kcal, Prt: 0 g, Fats: 0 g

3.8 Blackberry Mint Ice Tea

Time for cook: 15 minutes, **Complexity level:** easy, **Time for prep.:** 10 minutes, **Portions:** 4

Ingredients

- 6 fresh mint leaves
- 2 green tea bags
- Half a cup of fresh blackberries
- 3 cups of hot water

Directions

1. In a jug, add all ingredients & steep.
2. Strain & serve chilled.

Nutritional information

Carbs: 0 g, Cal: 8 kcal, Prt: 0 g, Fats: 0 g

3.9 Vegan Gelatin

Time for cook: 15 minutes, **Complexity level:** easy, **Time for prep.:** 10 minutes, **Portions:** 4

Ingredients

- 1 cup of any strained fruit juice
- Gelatin, as needed
- 1 cup of water
- 2 tbsp. of honey

Directions

1. In a pot, add all ingredients & put on a medium flame. Boil & stir as needed.
2. As it comes to a boil, add gelatin.
3. Mix well & turn the heat off.
4. Pour it into a bowl & let it set.
5. Serve chilled.
6. Add all the ingredients to a pot and slowly bring the mixture to a boil. Be sure you stir

Nutritional Information

Carbs: 15g, Cal: 60, Prt: 1g, Fats: 0g

3.10 Lemon and Pepper Tea

Time for cook: 5 minutes, **Complexity level:** easy, **Time for prep.:** 10 minutes, **Portions:** 1-2

Ingredients

- 1 1/2 tsp. of honey
- Half tsp. of turmeric powder
- 1 lemon juice
- 1/4 tsp. of black pepper

Directions

1. Add 2 cups of boiling water to a pot with all the ingredients.
2. Mix well & let it steep for a few minutes.
3. Strain if needed, & serve.

Nutritional information

Carbs: 1 g, Cal: 9 kcal, Prt: 1 g, Fats: 0 g

3.11 Mint Tea

Time for cook: 5 minutes, **Complexity level:** easy, **Time for prep.:** 10 minutes, **Portions:** 1

Ingredients

- 1 sprig of rosemary
- 10 mint leaves
- 1 tsp. of lemon juice

Directions

1. Add all ingredients to one cup of boiling water.
2. Steep for a few minutes, strain & serve.

Nutritional information

Carbs: 1 g, Cal: 5 kcal, Prt: 1 g, Fats: 0 g

3.12 Iced Peach Ginger Tea

Time for cook: 5 minutes, **Complexity level:** easy, **Time for prep.:** 10 minutes, **Portions:** 1

Ingredients

- 1/4 cup of peach slices
- 1-2 green tea bags
- 2-3 Ginger coins
- 1 ½ cups of boiling water

Directions

1. Add all ingredients to a jug.
2. Let it steep for 15 minutes. Strain & serve.
3. Serve chilled.

Nutritional information

Carbs: 1 g, Cal: 10 kcal, Prt: 1 g, Fats: 0 g

3.13 Anti-Inflammatory Golden Tonic

Time for cook: 5 minutes, **Complexity level:** easy, **Time for prep.:** 10 minutes, **Portions:** 4

Ingredients

- 2 bags of green tea
- 5 sprigs of fresh thyme
- 4 cups of water
- 1 piece of (2") peeled ginger, grated
- Ice cubes, as needed
- 1 piece of (2") peeled turmeric, grated
- 1 tbsp. of honey
- 1 tbsp. of cider vinegar

Directions

1. In a pan, add 2 cups of water & boil.
2. Add all the ingredients & simmer on low flame for 15 minutes.
3. Strain & keep it in the fridge.
4. Add the rest of the water or more if desired.
5. Serve.

Nutritional information

Carbs: 0 g, Cal: 5 kcal, Prt: 1 g, Fats: 0 g

3.14 Sugar-Free Decaf Fruit Punch

Time for cook: 5 minutes, **Complexity level:** easy, **Time for prep.:** 10 minutes, **Portions:** 4

Ingredients

- Water, 8 cups
- 4 tea bags of Decaffeinated Fruit Tea
- Stevia, as needed

Directions

1. In a pan, add water & boil.
2. Add tea bags & steep for 15 minutes.
3. Remove the tea bags. Add stevia as per your taste, and serve after chilling.

Nutritional information

Carbs: 1 g, Cal: 9 kcal, Prt: 1 g, Fats: 0 g

3.15 Lavender Lemonade

Time for cook: 0 minutes, **Complexity level:** easy, **Time for prep.:** 10 minutes, **Portions:** 4

Ingredients

- 1 tbsp. of Lavender Syrup
- 1 tbsp. of Lemonade powder
- 8 oz. of cold water

Directions

1. In a glass, add all ingredients, mix well & serve.

Nutritional information

Carbs: 3 g, Cal: 20 kcal, Prt: 0 g, Fats: 0 g

3.16 Strawberry Peach Jell-O

Time for cook: 5 minutes, **Complexity level:** easy, **Time for prep.:** 10 minutes, **Portions:** 4

Ingredients

- Sugar-Free Jell-O Strawberry, 1 pack
- 2 cups of water
- Sugar-Free Jell-O Peach, 1 pack

Directions

1. In a pan, add one cup of water & boil.
2. Turn the heat off, add one Jell-O packet, mix well & pour in a mold.
3. Keep it in the fridge and serve chilled.
4. Repeat the process with the second Jell-O packet.

Nutritional information

Carbs: 4 g, Cal: 25 kcal, Prt: 3 g, Fats: 4 g

3.17 Fresh Fruit Popsicles

Time for cook: 0 minutes, **Complexity level:** easy, **Time for prep.:** 10 minutes, **Portions:** 6

Ingredients

- 1/4 cup of blueberries
- 1 cup of coconut water
- 1/4 cup of chopped mangoes
- Half a cup of sliced strawberries
- 1/4 cup of sliced kiwi

Directions

1. Add the fruits to the molds equally.
2. Add the coconut water.
3. Freeze until done, and serve chilled. Do not eat the fruit chunks.

Nutritional information

Carbs: 10 g, Cal: 60 kcal, Prt: 6 g, Fats: 1 g

3.18 Coconut Lime Iced Tea

Time for cook: 5 minutes, **Complexity level:** easy, **Time for prep.:** 10 minutes, **Portions:** 6

Ingredients

- 3 cups of coconut water, heated
- 2 bags of black tea
- Half a lime, sliced thin

Directions

1. Add all ingredients to a jug.
2. Mix & let it steep for 15 minutes.
3. Strain & serve chilled.

Nutritional information

Carbs: 1 g, Cal: 9 kcal, Prt: 1 g, Fats: 0 g

3.19 Clear Protein Popsicles

Time for cook: 0 minutes, **Complexity level:** easy, **Time for prep.:** 10 minutes, **Portions:** 2-3

Ingredients

- 1 ½ cups of water
- Half a cup of raspberries
- 1 scoop of Clear Vegan Protein
- Half a cup of sliced strawberries

Directions

1. Mix the protein & water well.
2. Add fruits to the popsicle molds.
3. Add the protein water.
4. Set in the freezer, and serve when chilled. Do not eat the fruits.

Nutritional information

Carbs: 7 g, Cal: 30 kcal, Prt: 6 g, Fats: 6 g

3.20 Energy Drink

Time for cook: 10 minutes, **Complexity level:** easy, **Time for prep.:** 10 minutes, **Portions:** 1

Ingredients

- 2 bags of green tea
- 2 tbsp. of lemon juice
- 1 yerba tea bag
- 1 cup of boiling water
- 1 ½ tbsp. of honey
- Ice cubes, as needed

Directions

1. In a cup, add boiling water.
2. Add tea bags & steep for 5 minutes; take the tea bags out.
3. Add lemon juice, ice cubes & sweetener. Mix well & serve chilled.

Nutritional information

Carbs: 26 g, Cal: 97 kcal, Prt: 0 g, Fats: 0 g

3.21 Minty Watermelon Popsicles

Time for cook: 0 minutes, **Complexity level:** easy, **Time for prep.:** 10 minutes, **Portions:** 2-3

Ingredients

- 1 tbsp. of fresh mint leaves
- 1 tbsp. of honey
- 1 ½ cups of coconut water
- 2 1/2 cups of watermelon slices
- 2 tbsp. of lime juice

Directions

1. Add all ingredients to a blender.
2. Add to the popsicle molds. Keep them in the freezer.
3. Serve chilled.

Nutritional information

Carbs: 9 g, Cal: 40 kcal, Prt: 4 g, Fats: 5 g

3.22 Coconut Lime

Time for cook: 0 minutes, **Complexity level:** easy, **Time for prep.:** 10 minutes, **Portions:** 2-3

Ingredients

- 14 oz. of coconut water
- Lime zest, 2 tsp.
- Honey, to taste
- Lime juice, ¼ cup

Directions

1. Add all ingredients to a bowl, mix & pour in the molds.
2. Serve chilled.

Nutritional information

Carbs: 8 g, Cal: 21 kcal, Prt: 7 g, Fats: 0 g

3.23 Berry Lemon

Time for cook: 0 minutes, **Complexity level:** easy, **Time for prep.:** 10 minutes, **Portions:** 2-3

Ingredients

- 2 Tbsp. of lemon juice
- Half a cup of orange juice
- 2-4 Tbsp. of honey
- 1 ½ cup of fresh berries
- 1 Tbsp. of lemon zest

Directions

1. Add all ingredients to a blender.
2. Pulse until well combined.
3. Add to molds, and serve chilled.

Nutritional information

Carbs: 10 g, Cal: 47 kcal, Prt: 7 g, Fats: 9 g

3.24 Orange Mango Coconut Popsicles

Time for cook: 0 minutes, **Complexity level:** easy, **Time for prep.:** 10 minutes, **Portions:** 2-3

Ingredients

- 3 cups of mango
- 3 tbsp. of honey
- 2 cups of coconut water
- 3 tbsp. of orange juice

Directions

1. Add all ingredients to a blender.
2. Pulse until well combined.
3. Add to molds, and serve chilled.

Nutritional information

Carbs: 10 g, Cal: 50 kcal, Prt: 9 g, Fats: 12 g

3.25 Rainbow Fruit

Time for cook: 0 minutes, **Complexity level:** easy, **Time for prep.:** 10 minutes, **Portions:** 2-3

Ingredients

- 2-4 tbsp. of honey
- 1 cup of sliced mixed fruit
- 1 ½ cups of coconut water

Directions

1. Add fruits to the popsicle molds with the rest of the ingredients.
2. Keep it in the freezer until set.
3. Serve chilled.

Nutritional information

Carbs: 12 g, Cal: 45 kcal, Prt: 6 g, Fats: 5 g

3.26 Lavender-Chamomile Herbal Tea

Time for cook: 5 minutes, **Complexity level:** easy, **Time for prep.:** 10 minutes, **Portions:** 1

Ingredients

- Half tsp. of dried lavender
- Half tsp. of dried mint
- 1 tsp. of dried chamomile
- 1 cup of boiling water

Directions

1. Add all ingredients to a jug.
2. Mix & let it steep for 5-10 minutes.
3. Strain & serve.

Nutritional information

Carbs: 0 g, Cal: 3 kcal, Prt: 0 g, Fats: 1 g

3.27 Chicken clear Broth

Time for cook: 3 hours, **Complexity level:** easy, **Time for prep.:** 10 minutes, **Portions:** 4

Ingredients

- 20 cups of Water
- 10 sprigs of parsley
- 3 dried bay leaves
- Garlic, 2 cloves
- 3 carrots, cut in half
- 2 onions, cut into fours without peeling
- 4 stalks of Celery
- 5 lb. of chicken Bones

Directions

1. In a large pot, add water & chicken bones.
2. Boil & simmer with the rest of the ingredients for 3 hours.
3. Strain & serve.

Nutritional information

Carbs: 3 g, Cal: 10 kcal, Prt: 7 g, Fats: 3 g

3.28 Hibiscus-Pomegranate Iced Tea

Time for cook: 0 minutes, **Complexity level:** easy, **Time for prep.:** 10 minutes, **Portions:** 8

Ingredients

- 4 cups of cold water
- 4 cups of boiling water
- 1/4 cup of loose hibiscus tea
- 1 cup of pomegranate juice

Directions

1. Add the loose tea & steep in boiling water for 3- 5 minutes.
2. Mix pomegranate juice with water (cold.). Add to the strained tea, and serve with ice cubes.

Nutritional information

Carbs: 5 g, Cal: 19 kcal, Prt: 1 g, Fats: 0 g

3.29 Vegetable Clear Soup

Time for cook: 1-2 hours, **Complexity level:** easy, **Time for prep.:** 10 minutes, **Portions:** 4

Ingredients

- 1 tbsp. of Oregano
- 1 carrot
- Half a Stick of Celery
- 1 onion
- Half stick of Leek
- Salt, to-taste
- 5 Mushrooms

Directions

1. Add all ingredients to a large pot of water.
2. Boil & simmer for 1-2 hours.
3. Add salt, strain & serve.

Nutritional information

Carbs: 1 g, Cal: 19 kcal, Prt: 2 g, Fats: 2 g

3.30 Orange-Earl Grey Iced Tea

Time for cook: 10 minutes, **Complexity level:** easy, **Time for prep.:** 10 minutes, **Portions:** 8

Ingredients

- 1 orange peel
- ¼ cup of stevia
- 4 cups of boiling water
- 1/4 cup of loose Earl Grey tea
- ¾ cup of orange juice
- 4 cups of cold water

Directions

1. In boiling water, add the loose tea with orange peel & steep for 3-5 minutes.
2. Strain & add the rest of the ingredients.
3. Add cold water. Serve chilled.

Nutritional information

Carbs: 9 g, Cal: 35 kcal, Prt: 1 g, Fats: 0 g

3.31 Clear Broth

Time for cook: 2-3 hours, **Complexity level:** easy, **Time for prep.:** 10 minutes, **Portions:** 4

Ingredients

- Water, as needed
- Half a pound of Meat bones

Directions

1. Wash the bones well. Add to a pot with enough water to cover them.
2. Cook for 2-3 hours; keep adding water if it is running out.
3. Strain & serve.

Nutritional information

Carbs: 8 g, Cal: 45 kcal, Prt: 9 g, Fats: 4 g

3.32 Clear Apple Juice

Time for cook: 2-3 hours, **Complexity level:** easy, **Time for prep.:** 10 minutes, **Portions:** 8

Ingredients

- 3 Apples
- 3 cups of Water
- 3 tbsp. of stevia

Directions

1. Add apples to warm water & soak for half an hour.
2. Peel & slice the apples. Add to the pan with stevia.
3. Add water and cook for half an hour on medium flame.
4. Mash & cook for a few minutes more.
5. Strain & serve.

Nutritional information

Carbs: 7 g, Cal: 23 kcal, Prt: 3 g, Fats: 1 g

3.33 Strained Carrot Juice

Time for cook: 0 minutes, **Complexity level:** easy, **Time for prep.:** 10 minutes, **Portions:** 4-5

Ingredients
- Half a pound of carrots

Directions
1. Add carrots chunks to a blender with enough water to make juice.
2. Do it in stages; strain with a cheese cloth.
3. Serve cold.

Nutritional information

Carbs: 17 g, Cal: 79 kcal, Prt: 3 g, Fats: 0.8 g

3.34 Iced Mint Green Tea

Time for cook: 10 minutes, **Complexity level:** easy, **Time for prep.:** 10 minutes, **Portions:** 4

Ingredients
- 3 green tea bags
- 2 tbsp. of honey
- Half a cup of fresh mint leaves
- 4 cups of boiling water

Directions
1. In boiling water, add all ingredients, mix & let it steep for 5-7 minutes.
2. Strain & serve with ice.

Nutritional information

Carbs: 11 g, Cal: 76 kcal, Prt: 1 g, Fats: 0 g

3.35 Orange-Ginger Tea

Time for cook: 0 minutes, **Complexity level:** easy, **Time for prep.:** 10 minutes, **Portions:** 4

Ingredients
- ¼ cup of orange juice
- 4 green tea bags
- 4 cups of water
- 1 piece of (1") peeled ginger & sliced

Directions
1. In boiling water, add ginger & tea bags.
2. Turn the heat off & let it steep for 5 minutes.
3. Take the tea bags out & add orange juice.
4. Serve chilled.

Nutritional information

Carbs: 3 g, Cal: 11 kcal, Prt: 0 g, Fats: 0 g

3.36 Japanese Clear Soup

Time for cook: 1-2 hours, **Complexity level:** easy, **Time for prep.:** 10 minutes, **Portions:** 2-4

Ingredients
- 3 ½ cups of clear chicken broth
- 1 1/2 scallions, diced
- ¼ tsp. of sesame oil
- 1 ¾ cups of water
- 1/4 large, sweet onion, cut into chunks
- 2-3 cloves of garlic, smashed
- Salt, to taste
- 1 carrot, cut into chunks
- ¼" piece of fresh ginger, sliced
- 1 ¾ cup of clear beef broth
- 4 button mushrooms, thinly sliced

Directions
1. In a large pan, add oil, onion, ginger, carrots & garlic. Sauté the vegetables for a few minutes.
2. Add all the liquids, and let it come to a boil. Turn the heat low & simmer for 60 minutes.
3. Add salt to your taste.
4. Strain & serve.

Nutritional information

Carbs: 5 g, Cal: 46 kcal, Prt: 3 g, Fats: 1 g

Chapter 4: Full Liquid Purees

4.1 Roasted Garlic Soup

Time for cook: 20 mins, **Complexity level:** difficult, **Time for prep.:** 1 hr, **Portions:** 6

Ingredients

- Garlic 5 heads
- Carrots chopped 2
- Onion chopped ½
- Bone broth 1 ½ quarts
- Celery chopped 3 stalks
- Sea salt/pepper as required

Directions

1. Trim the tops off the garlic heads and roast for an hour at 325°F while gently brushing butter or coconut oil over the cut end.
2. Fry the onion, celery, carrot, and celery root in a deep fryer with a little bit of sea salt.
3. Add the liquid and garlic to the air fryer, then cook for 5 to 10 minutes at 350 F.
4. Season the soup with salt and pepper and blend it in a blender.

Nutritional information

Carbs: 11 g, Cal: 70 kcal, Prt: 6.8 g, Fats: 0.1 g

4.2 Lemon Vanilla Bean Custard

Time for cook: 5 mins, **Complexity level:** easy, **Time for prep.:** 10-12 mins, **Portions:** 4

Ingredients

- Full-fat coconut milk 240 ml
- Eggs 2
- Honey ¼ cup
- Fresh lemon zest 2 tsp
- Fresh lemon juice 2 tbsp
- Pure vanilla extract ½ tsp
- Vanilla bean paste ½ tsp
- Powdered gelatin (dissolved in water) 1 ½ tsp
- Sea salt 1 pinch

Directions

1. Combine the coconut milk, eggs, honey, lemon juice, lemon zest, vanilla bean paste, and sea salt in an air fryer set to 350°F for three minutes. After adding the dissolved gelatin, cook for 1 minute while continuously stirring.
2. The custard should be strained into a plate with a fine-mesh strainer, covered with plastic wrap, and chilled overnight.
3. Puree the custard in a food processor until it is silky-smooth.

Nutritional information

Carbs: 22 g, Cal: 254 kcal, Prt: 6.9 g, Fats: 16.9 g

4.3 Strawberry Greek Yogurt Whip

Time for cook: 0 mins, **Complexity level:** easy, **Time for prep.:** 10 mins, **Portions:** 6

Ingredients

- No calorie sweetener, about 1 tbsp
- Frozen strawberries 3
- Whipped topping about 1/2 cup
- Greek yogurt 2/3 of a cup

Directions

1. Place frozen strawberries in a small microwaveable bowl. Let them defrost for 60 seconds.
2. -In a bowl, use kitchen shears to slice the strawberries so that they are finely sliced and slightly runny.
3. Mix in Greek yogurt. Stir in the sweetener. Greek yogurt is beaten with a light topping and folded into the mixture. Serve right now or cover and chill until serving. Suitable for use as a yogurt dip or on its own.

Nutritional information

Carbs: 3 g, Cal: 24 kcal, Prt: 2 g, Fats: 1 g

4.4 Cucumber mint yogurt

Time for cook: 0 mins, **Complexity level:** easy, **Time for prep.:** 5 mins, **Portions:** 1

Ingredients

- Greek yogurt one cup
- Salt 1/8 tsp
- Cucumber 3 tbsp
- Green onion 1 tbsp
- Fresh mint leaves 1 tbsp

Directions

1. Put everything in a bowl and stir it up. Serve.

Nutritional information

Carbs: 8 g, Cal: 89 kcal, Prt: 15 g, Fats: 0 g

4.5 Raspberry Vinaigrette

Time for cook: 0 mins, **Complexity level:** easy, **Time for prep.:** 5 mins, **Portions:** 2

Ingredients

- Olive oil ½ cup
- Fresh basil ¼ cup
- Balsamic vinegar ½ cup
- Honey 2 tbsp
- Raspberries ½ cup

Directions

- Balsamic vinegar, honey, raspberries, and basil should be mixed well for one minute together in the food processor. Olive oil should be added to the mixer while running in a slow, constant stream until the dressing gets smooth.
- Serve atop a salad or with raw vegetables.

Nutritional information

Carbs: 5.2 g, Cal: 75 kcal, Prt: 27 g, Fats: 2.8 g

4.6 Cucumber Sauce

Time for cook: 0 mins, **Complexity level:** easy, **Time for prep.:** 5-7 mins, **Portions:** 2

Ingredients

- English cucumber 1
- Black pepper tastewise
- Milk yogurt 1 cup
- Kosher salt tastewise
- Garlic 2 cloves
- Chopped fresh dill 2 tbsp
- Lemon zest is 1 tsp plus fresh lemon juice 1 tbsp

Directions

1. The cucumber should be peeled and grated into a medium dish. Squeeze off most of its excess water with your hands into a basin or sink for disposing of.
2. Mix the yogurt, lemon zest, cucumber, dill, garlic, and lemon juice in a shallow dish.
3. Add more salt and pepper to taste after adding 1 tsp salt and 1/2 tsp pepper.
4. Serve your grilled fish or meat with a spoon.

Nutritional information

Carbs: 1 g, Cal: 20 kcal, Prt: 3 g, Fats: 0 g

4.7 Sugar-Free Applesauce

Time for cook: 4 hrs, **Complexity level:** easy, **Time for prep.:** 10 mins, **Portions:** 4

Ingredients

- Water ½ cup
- Apples 8
- Lemon juice 2 tbsp
- Cinnamon ½ tsp

Directions

1. Apples should be peeled and cored. To complete the task more quickly, use a paring knife. Reduce in size by chopping.
2. Apples should be added to the slow cooker. Put some cinnamon on top. To blend, stir. Include a half cup of water.
3. Cook the apples in your slow cooker on high for four hours or till they are soft. Lemon juice is added.
4. If your applesauce's texture is more chunky than you want, mash using a potato masher and mix it in an immersion blender. Serve hot or cold.

Nutritional information

Carbs: 18 g, Cal: 48 kcal, Prt: 23 g, Fats: 1.5 g

4.8 Chimichurri chicken Puree

Time for cook: 13 mins, **Complexity level:** easy, **Time for prep.:** 13 mins, **Portions:** 5

Ingredients

- Lean ground chicken ½ lb
- Apple cider vinegar 2 tsp
- Paprika ½ tsp
- Garlic peeled 2 cloves
- Dried oregano ¼ tsp
- Cilantro 2 tbsp
- Parsley ¼ cup

Directions

1. 2 Tbsp water should be heated over a moderate flame in a sauté pan. Add chicken, oregano, and paprika. Cook over six to eight minutes, breaking up any clumps as you go. To prevent the pan from drying out, put 1 Tbsp of water simultaneously as it evaporates.
2. Combine parsley, apple cider vinegar, cilantro, and three tablespoons of water and garlic together in a blender. To finely chop, pulse many times.
3. Stir the chimichurri into the pan to coat.
4. Process once more in the food processor till smooth.

Nutritional information

Carbs: 5 g, Cal: 47.6 kcal, Prt: 5.6 g, Fats: 2.3 g

4.9 Italian chicken puree

Time for cook: 0 mins, **Complexity level:** easy, **Time for prep.:** 5 mins, **Portions:** 1

Ingredients

- Canned chicken 1/4 cup
- Italian seasoning 1 tsp
- Tomato sauce 1 1/2 tbsp
- Pepper 1/8 tsp
- Salt 1/8 tsp

Directions

1. Combine everything in a mini food processor and pulse till smooth and creamy.
2. Put the bowl in the microwave for thirty seconds.
3. For an optional alternative, make a lasagna-style dish by adding cottage cheese (low fat) or ricotta cheese.

Nutritional information

Carbs: 3 g, Cal: 106 kcal, Prt: 13 g, Fats: 4 g

4.10 Chocolate Chip & Cherry Ice Cream

Time for cook: 0 mins, **Complexity level:** easy, **Time for prep.:** 10 mins, **Portions:** 1

Ingredients

- Unsweetened almond milk 1/2 cup
- Cherries, fresh 2 cups
- Chocolate chips 3 tbsp
- Banana 1/2

Directions

1. Remove all the cherry pits before washing and drying them. Place together in a glass container or freezer bag, then freeze for at least three hours. You may use frozen cherries if you lack the time.
2. Half of a banana should be frozen after being peeled.
3. Save the leftover almond milk cup and pour it into ice cube trays. Freeze them for a minimum of three hours.
4. Blend the frozen cherries, almond milk cubes, 1⁄2 a frozen banana, and ¼ cup almond milk for several minutes until smooth and creamy.
5. Add the chocolate chips, and then immediately enjoy.

Nutritional information

Carbs: 22.3 g, Cal: 126 kcal, Prt: 2.1 g, Fats: 4 g

4.11 Chocolate Coconut Protein Latte

Time for cook: 0 minutes, **Complexity level:** easy, **Time for prep.:** 10 minutes, **Portions:** 1-2

Ingredients

- Creamer, 2 Tbsp.
- Protein Powder, chocolate, 1 scoop
- Vanilla Syrup, without sugar, 1 tbsp.
- Coconut oil, 2 drops
- Black Coffee, 8 oz.
- Hazelnut Syrup, without sugar, 1 tbsp.

Directions

- In a large mug, add syrups, protein powder, creamer & oil. Mix until smooth.
- Add coffee & mix well serve chilled.

Nutritional information

Carbs: 5 g, Cal: 173 kcal, Prt: 22 g, Fats: 7 g

4.12 Shrimp Scampi Puree

Time for cook: 5 minutes, **Complexity level:** easy, **Time for prep.:** 10 minutes, **Portions:** 4

Ingredients

- 2 minced cloves of garlic
- 1 tbsp. of Olive oil
- 1 tbsp. of yogurt
-
- Half lb. of Shrimp
- ⅛ cup of chopped Parsley

Directions

1. Add oil to a pan on medium flame.
2. Add shrimp & cook for 2-3 minutes.
3. Add garlic & sauté for 60 seconds.
4. Turn the heat off & add parsley & yogurt. Mix well.
5. Add to a food processor & pulse until smooth.
6. Serve with a sprinkle of salt.

Nutritional information

Carbs: 1 g, Cal: 91 kcal, Prt: 14 g, Fats: 3.7 g

4.13 Spaghetti Squash Au Gratin

Time for cook: 25 minutes, **Complexity level:** easy, **Time for prep.:** 20 minutes, **Portions:** 8

Ingredients

- 2 tbsp. of olive oil
- 3/4 cup of yogurt
- 1 chopped onion
- 1 cup of cheddar cheese, shredded
- 1 spaghetti squash, medium
- 1 tsp. of red pepper flakes
- 1/4 tsp. of garlic powder

Directions

1. Let the oven preheat to 375 F.
2. Slice the squash in half & take the seeds out.
3. Add half-inch of water in 2 dishes, add every half in each dish & microwave until tender or for 10 to 14 minutes.
4. In a bowl, add garlic powder, red pepper flakes & onion. Mix.
5. Add oil to a pan on medium flame
6. Add onion mixture, and sauté until browned.
7. With a fork, scrape the squash into spaghetti. Add the cheese, sautéed onion & yogurt. Mix well.
8. Transfer to a baking dish, add cheese & bake for 20 minutes at 375 F.

Nutritional information

Carbs: 7 g, Cal: 115 kcal, Prt: 7 g, Fats: 7 g

4.14 Butternut Squash Soup

Time for cook: 30 minutes, **Complexity level:** easy, **Time for prep.:** 15 minutes, **Portions:** 10-13

Ingredients

- Half a cup of diced onion
- 1 cup of chopped celery
- ¼ cup of maple syrup
- 1 cup of diced carrot
- ¼ cup of butter
- 1 lb. of peeled butternut squash, chopped
- 4 cups of water
- ⅛ tsp. of black pepper
- Half tsp. of apple cider vinegar
- ¼ cup of brown sugar
- ¼ tsp. of pumpkin pie spice
- 1 ½ tsp. of sea salt
- 2 cups of heavy cream
- Half tsp. of vanilla extract
- 1 tsp. of ground cinnamon

Directions

1. In a pot, add butter, carrots, onion & celery. Sauté for 8 minutes.
2. Add salt, pepper, cinnamon, butternut squash, & pumpkin spice, and cook for a few seconds.
3. Add sugar, water & maple syrup. Mix well & let it come to a boil.
4. Simmer on low flame for 15 minutes or until squash becomes soft.
5. Puree the soup with a stick blender.
6. Add vinegar, cream & vanilla, and whisk well.
7. Adjust seasoning & serve.

Nutritional information

Carbs: 10 g, Cal: 177 kcal, Prt: 4 g, Fats: 14 g

4.15 Apple Pie Protein Shake

Time for cook: 0 minutes, **Complexity level:** easy, **Time for prep.:** 10 minutes, **Portions:** 1

Ingredients

- Vanilla Protein Powder, 1 scoop
- Ice Cubes, as needed
- 1 cup of skim milk
- 1 pouch of Apple Cider Hot Mix
- 1/8 tsp. of Cinnamon

Directions

1. Add all ingredients to a blender and pulse until smooth.

Nutritional information

Carbs: 20 g, Cal: 188 kcal, Prt: 21 g, Fats: 0 g

4.16 Shamrock Protein Shake

Time for cook: 0 minutes, **Complexity level:** easy, **Time for prep.:** 10 minutes, **Portions:** 1

Ingredients

- 2 scoops of Vanilla High Protein
- 1 cup of spinach
- 1 cup of almond milk, unsweetened
- 1/4 tsp. of mint extract

Directions

- Add all ingredients to a blender.
- Pulse until smooth. Serve chilled.

Nutritional information

Carbs: 10 g, Cal: 180 kcal, Prt: 28 g, Fats: 5 g

4.17 Turkey Tacos with Refried Beans Puree

Time for cook: 20 minutes, **Complexity level:** easy, **Time for prep.:** 10 minutes, **Portions:** 1

Ingredients

- Half garlic clove, minced
- 1 tbsp. of chopped Cilantro
- Half cup of pinto beans, rinsed
- ⅛ cup of chicken broth

For turkey

- ⅛ tsp. of Paprika
- ⅛ tsp. of Mild chili powder
- ¼ lb. of Lean ground turkey
- ⅛ tsp. of Garlic powder
- ⅛ tsp. of Cumin

Directions

1. In a pan, add 2 tbsp. of water on medium flame.
2. Add garlic & cook for 1 minute; add broth & beans. Let it come to a boil.
3. Turn the heat low & simmer for 5 minutes. Mash with a masher & cook until all liquid is gone.
4. Turn the heat off & mix the cilantro.
5. Add all spices to a pan, & toast for 60 seconds.
6. Add turkey & 2 tbsp. of water, cook for 6 to 8 minutes.
7. After the water has evaporated, add one tbsp. of water.
8. Transfer to a food processor with beans, pulse until smooth.
9. Serve.

Nutritional information

Carbs: 5 g, Cal: 69 kcal, Prt: 10.7 g, Fats: 0.9 g

4.18 Pureed Chicken Salad

Time for cook: 0 minutes, **Complexity level:** easy, **Time for prep.:** 10 minutes, **Portions:** 1

Ingredients

- 2 tbsp. of yogurt
- Black pepper, a pinch
- 2 tbsp. of Light Mayonnaise
- ⅛ tsp. of celery salt
- 1 chicken breast, cooked
- ⅛ tsp. of onion powder

Directions

1. In a food processor, add chicken breast and pulse until smooth.
2. Mix with the rest of the ingredients.
3. Serve.

Nutritional information

Carbs: 1 g, Cal: 84 kcal, Prt: 10 g, Fats: 4 g

4.19 Pear & Ricotta Puree

Time for cook: 0 minutes, **Complexity level:** easy, **Time for prep.:** 10 minutes, **Portions:** 1

Ingredients

- 1/4 tsp. of cinnamon
- 2 tbsp. of yogurt
- 3 pieces of tinned pear (with no sugar)
- 4.4 oz. of ricotta
- Half tsp. of vanilla essence

Directions

1. In a food processor, add all the ingredients.
2. Pulse until smooth, and serve.

Nutritional information

Carbs: 7 g, Cal: 76 kcal, Prt: 6 g, Fats: 2 g

4.20 Black Bean And Lime Puree

Time for cook: 0 minutes, **Complexity level:** easy, **Time for prep.:** 10 minutes, **Portions:** 1

Ingredients

- 1 tbsp. of protein powder
- Half tbsp. of lime juice
- 1/4 cup of black beans, rinsed
- Half tbsp. juice from jarred jalapeños
- 1/4 cup of chicken broth

Directions

1. Add jalapenos juice, beans & lime juice, and place on medium flame in a pan.
2. Mix for 1-2 minutes.
3. Add broth & cook for a few minutes, then pulse with a stick blender until smooth.
4. Add protein powder after it has cooled down a bit.
5. Serve.

Nutritional information

Carbs: 10 g, Cal: 94 kcal, Prt: 10 g, Fats: 1 g

4.21 Roasted Red Pepper & Butter Bean Puree

Time for cook: 0 minutes, **Complexity level:** medium, **Time for prep.:** 40 minutes, **Portions:** 2-3

Ingredients

- 2 garlic cloves, without peeling
- 1 red pepper, whole
- 1/4 cup of water or more
- 1 grated carrot
- 1/4 cup of pine nuts
- 14 oz. tin of butter beans washed
- 2 tbsp. of olive oil
- 5.3 oz. of feta, crumbled
- Half to 1 tsp. of chili flakes
- 1 lemon's juice & zest
- Salt & pepper, to taste

Directions

1. Let the oven preheat to 350 F.
2. Place red pepper, pine nuts & garlic cloves on a parchment-lined baking sheet.
3. Roast for half an hour; take the pine nuts out after 7 to 8 minutes, and take the garlic out after 20 minutes.
4. Remove the charred skin of the pepper, seeds & stalk.
5. Peel the garlic, and transfer to a food processor with all the ingredients.
6. Pulse until smooth. Serve.

Nutritional information

Carbs: 12 g, Cal: 78 kcal, Prt: 18 g, Fats: 8 g

4.22 Red Pepper Enchilada Bean Puree

Time for cook: 10 minutes, **Complexity level:** easy, **Time for prep.:** 10 minutes, **Portions:** 1

Ingredients

- 1 1/2 tbsp. of red enchilada sauce
- Half cup of canned black beans, rinsed
- 2 tbsp. of chicken broth
- 1 tbsp. of protein powder
- 2 tbsp. of chopped jarred roasted red pepper

Directions

1. In a pan, add all ingredients (except for protein powder) to a pan. Place on medium heat.
2. Mix well, and pulse with a stick blender.
3. Let it cool for a few minutes, and add powder. Mix & serve.

Nutritional information

Carbs: 25 g, Cal: 25 kcal, Prt: 19 g, Fats: 1 g

4.23 Melon Shake

Time for cook: 0 minutes, **Complexity level:** easy, **Time for prep.:** 10 minutes, **Portions:** 1

Ingredients

- 1/4 cantaloupe, chunks
- 3 to 4 ice cubes
- Half a cup of yogurt
- 1/4 cup of milk

Directions

1. Add all ingredients to a blender.
2. Pulse until smooth & serve.

Nutritional information

Carbs: 1 g, Cal: 9 kcal, Prt: 3 g, Fats: 2 g

4.24 Leek & Potato Soup

Time for cook: 20 minutes, **Complexity level:** easy, **Time for prep.:** 10 minutes, **Portions:** 6

Ingredients

- 2 tbsp. of olive oil
- 2 potatoes, peeled & cubed
- 2-3 leeks, chopped & cleaned
- 1 onion, chopped
- 1-2 tbsp. of butter
- 6 cups of chicken broth
- Salt & Pepper, to taste

Directions

1. In a large pot, add oil & butter.
2. Add leeks & onion, and sauté on a medium flame for 5-6 minutes.
3. Add broth & simmer. Add potatoes, and cook until soft.
4. Season as per your taste.
5. Pulse with a stick blender.
6. Add a splash of milk if you like, or serve it as it is.

Nutritional information

Carbs: 25 g, Cal: 262 kcal, Prt: 9 g, Fats: 6 g

4.25 Jell-O Mousse

Time for cook: 20 minutes, **Complexity level:** easy, **Time for prep.:** 10 minutes, **Portions:** 4

Ingredients

- 1 container of Jell-O Sugar-Free
- 2 scoops of Whey Protein
- Half a cup of water
- 10.6 oz. of Yogurt

Directions

1. In a pan, add water & heat.
2. Add the jell- O & mix well. Turn the heat off.
3. Add the rest of the ingredients, mix & add to ramekins.
4. Serve when it is set.

Nutritional information

Carbs: 5 g, Cal: 105 kcal, Prt: 20 g, Fats: 0 g

4.26 Mexican Egg Puree

Time for cook: 10 minutes, **Complexity level:** easy, **Time for prep.:** 10 minutes, **Portions:** 4

Ingredients

- 3 Eggs
- Half tbsp. of yogurt
- 1 tbsp. of Cilantro, chopped
- Half tsp. of Cumin
- ¼ lb. of Loose turkey sausage
- ¼ tsp. of Paprika
- ⅛ cup. of canned black beans, rinsed

Directions

1. Whisk eggs with paprika, yogurt, & cumin.
2. Cook turkey in a pan for 5 to 6 minutes until done.
3. Turn the heat to low, add eggs & stir for 2 to 3 minutes.
4. Add beans & cook for 60 seconds. Pulse with a stick blender after adding cilantro.
5. Add 2 tbsp. of water if required.
6. Serve.

Nutritional information

Carbs: 2.7 g, Cal: 128 kcal, Prt: 12 g, Fats: 7 g

4.27 Strawberry Banana Protein Sorbet

Time for cook: 0 minutes, **Complexity level:** easy, **Time for prep.:** 10 minutes, **Portions:** 1

Ingredients

- 2 1/2 tbsp. of almond milk, unsweetened
- 1/4 tsp. of vanilla extract
- 1 banana, sliced & frozen
- 3 tbsp. of Strawberry Banana Meal Replacement
- 1 cup of frozen strawberries

Directions

1. Add all ingredients to a blender.
2. Pulse until smooth.
3. Serve.

Nutritional information

Carbs: 10 g, Cal: 55 kcal, Prt: 4 g, Fats: 5 g

4.28 Avocado & Edamame Smash

Time for cook: 5 minutes, **Complexity level:** easy, **Time for prep.:** 10 minutes, **Portions:** 4

Ingredients

- 1/4 cup of fresh basil leaves
- 1/4 tsp. of chili flakes
- 1 avocado
- 1.7 oz. of feta, crumbled
- Half cup of edamame beans, shelled & frozen
- 1/4 tsp. of garlic powder
- 1 tsp. of lemon zest
- 1 lemon juice
- Salt & pepper to taste

Directions

1. Add edamame beans to boiling water for 5 minutes. Drain & wash with cold water.
2. Add all ingredients to a food processor and pulse until smooth.
3. Serve.

Nutritional information

Carbs: 21 g, Cal: 78 kcal, Prt: 8 g, Fats: 3 g

4.29 Scrambled Eggs With Black Bean Puree

Time for cook: 8 minutes, **Complexity level:** easy, **Time for prep.:** 10 minutes, **Portions:** 4

Ingredients

For eggs

- 1/8 tsp. of each salt & pepper
- 1 egg

Black Bean Puree

- 1 tbsp. of whey protein powder
- 3 tbsp. of green enchilada sauce
- Half cup of canned black beans, rinsed
- 2 tbsp. of chicken broth

Directions

1. In a pan, add beans on a medium flame.
2. Add sauce & cook for 2 minutes; add broth.
3. Puree with a stick blender. Cool for a few minutes; add protein powder & mix.
4. Cook egg with salt & pepper. Serve with black bean puree.

Nutritional information

Carbs: 6 g, Cal: 118 kcal, Prt: 11 g, Fats: 5 g

4.30 Strawberry Cheesecake Shake

Time for cook: 0 minutes, **Complexity level:** easy, **Time for prep.:** 10 minutes, **Portions:** 4

Ingredients

- Half a cup of yogurt
- 1/4 cup of cream cheese
- 4 to 5 fresh strawberries
- Ice cubes, as needed

Directions

1. Add all ingredients to a blender.
2. Pulse until smooth.
3. Serve.

Nutritional information

Carbs: 9 g, Cal: 59 kcal, Prt: 4 g, Fats: 4 g

4.31 Tomato Tarragon Soup

Time for cook: 20 minutes, **Complexity level:** easy, **Time for prep.:** 10 minutes, **Portions:** 4

Ingredients

- 1 onion, chopped
- 28 oz. of canned tomatoes
- Half tsp. of black pepper
- 2 tbsp. of olive oil
- 15 oz. of canned diced tomatoes
- 1 tbsp. of fresh tarragon
- 1 tsp. of salt
- Half a cup of sour cream

Directions

1. Heat the olive oil on a medium flame, and sauté the onion until translucent.
2. Add tomatoes with juices, salt & pepper.
3. Simmer for 10 minutes, and puree with a stick blender.
4. Turn the heat low & add tarragon & sour cream.
5. Serve.

Nutritional information

Carbs: 16 g, Cal: 188 kcal, Prt: 4 g, Fats: 13 g

4.32 PB Banana Protein Shake

Time for cook: 0 minutes, **Complexity level:** easy, **Time for prep.:** 10 minutes, **Portions:** 1

Ingredients

- 1 scoop of Protein Powder
- 1 tbsp. of Peanut Butter Powder
- Half a cup of Skim Milk
- Small Banana
- Ice Cubes, as needed

Directions

1. Add all ingredients to a blender and pulse until smooth.
2. Serve.

Nutritional information

Carbs: 18 g, Cal: 171 kcal, Prt: 27 g, Fats: 1 g

4.33 Chicken & Black Bean Mole Puree

Time for cook: 20 minutes, **Complexity level:** easy, **Time for prep.:** 10 minutes, **Portions:** 4

Ingredients

- Half cup of canned black beans, rinsed
- 1 ½ tbsp. of soaked almonds
- ⅛ tsp. of coriander
- ¼ lb. of lean ground chicken
- ⅛ tsp. of garlic powder
- ⅛ cup of chicken broth
- ¼ tbsp. of cacao powder
- Half Garlic clove, Minced
- ¼ tsp. of paprika
- ⅛ tsp. of dried oregano
- ⅛ tsp. of cumin
- 1 tbsp. of cilantro, chopped

Directions

1. Sauté garlic in 2 tbsp. of water for 60 seconds.
2. Add chicken & cook for 8 minutes; add one more tbsp. of water.
3. Add the rest of the ingredients to a blender. Pulse until smooth.
4. Add to the chicken & simmer until heat through.
5. Serve.

Nutritional information

Carbs: 9 g, Cal: 109 kcal, Prt: 19 g, Fats: 3.9 g

4.34 Pureed Salsa and Beans

Time for cook: 10 minutes, **Complexity level:** easy, **Time for prep.:** 10 minutes, **Portions:** 4

Ingredients

- 1 scoop of protein powder
- 2 tbsp. of salsa
- 1 can of (15 oz.) pinto beans
- 2 tbsp. of chicken broth

Directions

1. Add all ingredients to a pan & place on medium flame.
2. Cook until heated & puree with a stick blender.
3. Serve.

Nutritional information

Carbs: 15 g, Cal: 128 kcal, Prt: 11 g, Fats: 1 g

4.35 Milk Shake

Time 5or cook: 0 minutes, **Complexity level:** easy, **Time for prep.:** 10 minutes, **Portions:** 1

Ingredients

- Half a cup of milk
- Half a cup of ice cream

Directions

1. Add to the blender, pulse until smooth.
2. Serve.

Nutritional information

Carbs: 10 g, Cal: 91 kcal, Prt: 6 g, Fats: 4 g

4.36 Chia Avocado Chocolate Mousse

Time for cook: 0 minutes, **Complexity level:** easy, **Time for prep.:** 10 minutes, **Portions:** 1-2

Ingredients

- 1 avocado
- 2/3 cup of dark chocolate chips
- 1/4 tsp. of vanilla extract
- 2 tbsp. of chia seeds
- 1 can of (~14 oz.) coconut milk
- 2 tbsp. of maple syrup

Directions

1. In a blender, add all ingredients.
2. Pulse until smooth. Serve after freezing in the freezer.

Nutritional information

Carbs: 12 g, Cal: 101 kcal, Prt: 6 g, Fats: 10 g

4.37 Strawberry Chia Protein Smoothie

Time for cook: 0 minutes, **Complexity level:** easy, **Time for prep.:** 10 minutes, **Portions:** 4

Ingredients

- Half a cup of Frozen Strawberries
- Half a scoop of Protein Powder
- Half a cup of Soy Milk
- ¼ cup of Vanilla maple ice cream
- 0.5 oz. of chia seeds

Directions

1. Add to the blender, pulse until smooth.
2. Serve.

Nutritional information

Carbs: 24 g, Cal: 198 kcal, Prt: 1 g, Fats: 6 g

4.38 Turkish Tomato, Lentil & Mint Soup

Time for cook: 20 minutes, **Complexity level:** easy, **Time for prep.:** 10 minutes, **Portions:** 4

Ingredients

- 2 cups of Canned Lentils
- 1 clove of Garlic
- 14 oz. of canned Chopped Tomatoes
- 1 Onion, chopped
- 2 ½ cups of Vegetable Stock

Directions

1. Sauté the garlic & onion in a splash of oil for 3 to 5 minutes.
2. Add tomatoes & the rest of the ingredients.
3. Let it come to a boil, turn the heat low & simmer for 15 to 20 minutes.
4. Puree with a stick blender.
5. Serve.

Nutritional information

Carbs: 15 g, Cal: 97 kcal, Prt: 7 g, Fats: 1 g

4.39 Soft Crab Salad

Time for cook: 0 minutes, **Complexity level:** easy, **Time for prep.:** 10 minutes, **Portions:** 4

Ingredients

- 1 pinch of dried dill
- 1 tbsp. of light mayonnaise
- Half a scoop of protein powder
- 2 oz. of imitation crab
- 1 pinch of seafood seasoning

Directions

1. Cut the meat into small pieces.
2. Add protein & mayo, and mix well.
3. Add seasonings & serve.

Nutritional information

Carbs: 8 g, Cal: 118 kcal, Prt: 13 g, Fats: 5 g

4.40 Spaghetti Frappe

Time for cook: 0 minutes, **Complexity level:** easy, **Time for prep.:** 10 minutes, **Portions:** 1-2

Ingredients

- Half a cup of spaghetti sauce
- Grated Parmesan cheese, as needed
- 1/4 cup of cooked vegetables
- Half a cup of cooked spaghetti
- Milk, as needed

Directions

1. Add all ingredients to a blender, except for the cheese.
2. Pulse until smooth; add to a pan. Heat for 1 minute.
3. Serve with cheese on top.

Nutritional information

Carbs: g, Cal: 9 kcal, Prt: 1 g, Fats: 0 g

4.41 Curried Sweet Potato Soup

Time for cook: 20 minutes, **Complexity level:** easy, **Time for prep.:** 20 minutes, **Portions:** 6

Ingredients

- 1 yellow onion, chopped
- 2 tsp. of curry powder
- 4 cloves garlic, minced
- 4 to 6 cups of vegetable broth
- 2 peeled sweet potatoes, baked
- Salt, to taste
- Half tsp. of cumin
- 1/8 tsp. of cinnamon

Directions

1. Sauté the garlic & onion until tender in a splash of stock or water.
2. Add spices, garlic, onion & potato with 4 cups of broth in a pot, and simmer for a few minutes.
3. Puree with a stick blender.
4. Adjust seasoning & serve.

Nutritional information

Carbs: 14 g, Cal: 61 kcal, Prt: 1 g, Fats: 0 g

4.42 Carrot Ginger Soup

Time for cook: 20 minutes, **Complexity level:** medium, **Time for prep.:** 10 minutes, **Portions:** 4

Ingredients

- ⅔ cup of red split lentils
- 1 tsp. of turmeric
- 1 onion
- 4 tbsp. of coconut milk
- 3 tsp. of grated ginger
- 8 carrots, cut into chunks
- 6 cups of water
- Sea salt, a pinch

Directions

1. Sauté chopped onion in hot oil until translucent.
2. Add lentils & carrots, and cook for a few minutes.
3. Add the rest of the ingredients except for coconut milk.
4. Cook for 20 minutes, and turn the heat off.
5. Puree the soup with a stick blender. Add coconut milk, and cook until heated.
6. Adjust seasoning & serve.

Nutritional information

Carbs: 11 g, Cal: 120 kcal, Prt: 9 g, Fats: 10 g

4.43 Chicken "Noodle" Soup

Time for cook: 20 minutes, **Complexity level:** easy, **Time for prep.:** 10 minutes, **Portions:** 4

Ingredients

- 1 stalk of celery, diced
- Salt and pepper, to taste
- 1 carrot, diced
- 1 small zucchini, cut into matchsticks
- 4 to 5 cups of chicken broth
- 1 tbsp. of chicken bouillon granules

Directions

1. In a pot, add broth & boil. Add carrots & celery.
2. Simmer for 15 to 20 minutes.
3. Add the rest of the ingredients & cook for 5-7 minutes.
4. Serve.

Nutritional information

Carbs: 4 g, Cal: 68 kcal, Prt: 7 g, Fats: 2 g

4.44 Basic Tuna Salad

Time for cook: 0 minutes, **Complexity level:** easy, **Time for prep.:** 10 minutes, **Portions:** 1

Ingredients

- 1/4 tsp. of black pepper
- 2 tsp. of pickle juice
- 3 oz. of tuna in water, drained
- 1 tbsp. of mayonnaise

Directions

1. Mash the tuna, and mix it with the rest of the ingredients.
2. Adjust seasoning & serve.

Nutritional information

Carbs: 3 g, Cal: 89 kcal, Prt: 17 g, Fats: 1 g

4.45 Buffalo Chicken Salad

Time for cook: 0 minutes, **Complexity level:** easy, **Time for prep.:** 10 minutes, **Portions:** 1

Ingredients

- 1/4 cup of light mayo
- 5 stalks of celery
- Half tsp. of onion powder
- 2 cups of cooked & shredded seasoned chicken breast
- 3 tbsp. of buffalo sauce

Directions

1. Add all ingredients, except for celery stalks, to a bowl. Mix & serve with celery stalks.

Nutritional information

Carbs: 1 g, Cal: 104 kcal, Prt: 17 g, Fats: 1 g

4.46 Beet Hummus

Time for cook: 0 minutes, **Complexity level:** easy, **Time for prep.:** 10 minutes, **Portions:** 1

Ingredients

- 2 Tbsp. of Apple Cider Vinegar
- 1 garlic clove
- 2 Tbsp. of Sesame Tahini
- 1 lemon juice
- Water, 1 Tbsp.
- 1 Tbsp. of Ground Cumin,
- 1 Beet

Directions

1. Boil the beet for half an hour, then peel it.
2. Add all ingredients to a food processor. Pulse until smooth

Nutritional information

Carbs: 8 g, Cal: 84 kcal, Prt: 3 g, Fats: 5 g

4.47 Tuscan Tuna Salad

Time for cook: 0 minutes, **Complexity level:** easy, **Time for prep.:** 10 minutes, **Portions:** 4

Ingredients

- 2 tbsp. of chopped red onion
- 1/4 cup of Italian dressing, fat-free
- 2 tbsp. of fresh chopped parsley
- 2 cloves of garlic, minced
- 2 cans of tuna in water & drained
- 2 tbsp. of chopped roasted jarred red pepper
- 1 lemon's zest

Directions

1. In a bowl, add all ingredients & mix.
2. Serve.

Nutritional information

Carbs: 6 g, Cal: 81 kcal, Prt: 11 g, Fats: 1 g

4.48 Butternut Squash Soup with Thyme

Time for cook: 40 minutes, **Complexity level:** easy, **Time for prep.:** 10 minutes, **Portions:** 4

Ingredients

- 1 peeled Butternut Squash & cubed
- 2 Cloves of Garlic
- 4 Cups of vegetable stock
- Salt & Pepper, to taste
- 1 Tbsp. of olive oil
- ¼ to 1/5 Tsp. of cumin
- 1/4 Tsp. of nutmeg
- 3 to 4 Sprigs of Fresh Thyme
- Half Onion, diced
- 1/4 Tsp. of cinnamon

Directions

1. Sauté the thyme, onion & garlic in hot oil for 5 minutes.
2. Add squash & sauté for 1 minute.
3. Add stock & simmer for half an hour. Add seasonings & mix well.
4. Simmer for a few minutes more & turn the heat off.
5. Puree the soup with a stick blender.
6. Serve.

Nutritional information

Carbs: 26 g, Cal: 150 kcal, Prt: 2 g, Fats: 4 g

4.49 Fruit Smoothie

Time for cook: 40 minutes, **Complexity level:** easy, **Time for prep.:** 10 minutes, **Portions:** 1-2

Ingredients
- Ice cubes
- 3 to 4 fresh strawberries
- Half a cup of yogurt
- 1 Banana
- Half a cup of orange juice

Directions
1. Add all ingredients to a blender.
2. Pulse until smooth & serve.

Nutritional information

Carbs: 8 g, Cal: 29 kcal, Prt: 5 g, Fats: 2 g

4.50 Creamy Coconut Chia Pudding

Time for cook: 0 mins, **Complexity level:** easy, **Time for prep.:** 5 mins, **Portions:** 2

Ingredients
- 1 cup unsweetened coconut milk
- 1/4 cup chia seeds
- 1 tbsp honey or sweetener of choice
- 1/4 tsp vanilla extract
- Shredded coconut for garnish (optional)

Directions
1. Combine coconut milk, chia seeds, honey or sweetener, and vanilla extract in a bowl. Stir well.
2. Let the mixture sit for 10 minutes, then stir again to prevent clumping.
3. Refrigerate for at least 1 hour or overnight to allow the chia seeds to absorb the liquid and thicken.
4. Stir well before serving and garnish with shredded coconut, if desired.

Nutritional information

Carbs: 14 g, Cal: 190 kcal, Prt4 g, Fats: 14 g

4.51 Creamy Banana Protein Shake

Time for cook: 0 mins, **Complexity level:** easy, **Time for prep.:** 5 mins, **Portions:** 2

Ingredients
- 1 cup unsweetened almond milk
- 1 scoop of banana protein powder
- Ice cubes, as needed
- 1 ripe banana
- 1 tbsp almond butter

Directions
1. Combine almond milk, banana protein powder, ripe banana, and almond butter in a blender. Blend until smooth.
2. Add ice cubes and blend again until desired consistency is reached.
3. Serve chilled.

Nutritional information

Carbs: 12 g, Cal: 200 kcal, Prt: 25 g, Fats: 8 g

4.52 Creamy Pumpkin Soup

Time for cook: 20 mins, **Complexity level:** easy, **Time for prep.:** 5 mins, **Portions:** 2

Ingredients
- 1 cup canned pumpkin puree
- 1 cup vegetable broth
- 1/4 cup heavy cream
- 1/2 tsp pumpkin pie spice
- Salt and pepper to taste
- Pumpkin seeds for garnish (optional)

Directions
1. In a saucepan, combine pumpkin puree and vegetable broth. Cook over medium heat until heated through.
2. Stir in heavy cream, pumpkin pie spice, and season with salt and pepper.
3. Cook for about 15 minutes until flavors meld together.
4. Garnish with pumpkin seeds, if desired. Serve warm.

Nutritional information

Carbs: 10 g, Cal: 130 kcal, Prt2 g, Fats: 10 g

4.53 Blueberry Protein Smoothie

Time for cook: 0 mins, **Complexity level:** easy, **Time for prep.:** 5 mins, **Portions:** 2

Ingredients

- 1 cup unsweetened almond milk
- 1 scoop vanilla protein powder
- 1/2 cup frozen blueberries
- 1 tbsp almond butter
- Ice cubes, as needed

Directions

1. Combine almond milk, vanilla protein powder, frozen blueberries, and almond butter in a blender. Blend until smooth.
2. Add ice cubes and blend again until desired consistency is reached.
3. Serve chilled.

Nutritional information

Carbs: 10 g,Cal: 160 kcal, Prt20 g, Fats: 6 g

4.54 Creamy Spinach Soup

Time for cook: 15 mins, **Complexity level:** easy, **Time for prep.:** 5 mins, **Portions:** 2

Ingredients

- 2 cups fresh spinach leaves
- 1 cup vegetable broth
- 1/4 cup Greek yogurt
- 1 clove garlic, minced
- Salt and pepper to taste
- Nutmeg for garnish (optional)

Directions

1. In a saucepan, combine spinach and vegetable broth. Cook over medium heat until spinach wilts.
2. Remove from heat and let cool slightly. Transfer to a blender and blend until smooth.
3. Return the mixture to the saucepan and heat over low heat.
4. Stir in Greek yogurt and minced garlic and season with salt and pepper.
5. Cook for about 10 minutes, until heated through.
6. Garnish with a sprinkle of nutmeg, if desired. Serve warm.

Nutritional information

Carbs: 4 g,Cal: 70 kcal, Prt6 g, Fats: 2 g

4.55 Creamy Broccoli Soup

Time for cook: 15 mins, **Complexity level:** easy, **Time for prep.:** 5 mins, **Portions:** 2

Ingredients

- 2 cups broccoli florets
- 1 cup vegetable broth
- 1/4 cup heavy cream
- Salt and pepper to taste
- Grated cheddar cheese for garnish (optional)

Directions

1. Steam or boil the broccoli until tender.
2. In a blender, combine the cooked broccoli and vegetable broth. Blend until smooth.
3. Pour the mixture into a saucepan and heat over medium heat.
4. Stir in the heavy cream and season with salt and pepper.
5. Cook for about 10 minutes, until heated through.
6. Garnish with grated cheddar cheese, if desired. Serve warm.

Nutritional information

Carbs: 12 g,Cal: 150 kcal, Prt4 g, Fats: 10 g

4.56 Vanilla Protein Pudding

Time for cook: 0 mins, **Complexity level:** easy, **Time for prep.:** 5 mins, **Portions:** 2

Ingredients

- 1 scoop vanilla protein powder
- 1 cup unsweetened almond milk
- 1/4 tsp vanilla extract
- Sugar substitute to taste (optional)

Directions

1. Whisk together protein powder and almond milk in a bowl until well combined.
2. Stir in vanilla extract and sugar substitute, if desired.
3. Refrigerate for at least 30 minutes to allow the pudding to set.
4. Serve chilled.

Nutritional information

Carbs: 2 g,Cal: 100 kcal, Prt20 g, Fats: 2 g

4.57 Chocolate Mint Protein Smoothie

Time for cook: 0 mins, **Complexity level:** easy, **Time for prep.:** 5 mins, **Portions:** 2

Ingredients

- 1 cup unsweetened almond milk
- 1 scoop of chocolate protein powder
- 1/4 tsp peppermint extract
- 1 cup spinach
- Ice cubes, as needed

Directions

1. Combine almond milk, chocolate protein powder, peppermint extract, and spinach in a blender. Blend until smooth.
2. Add ice cubes and blend again until desired consistency is reached.
3. Serve chilled.

Nutritional information

Carbs: 6 g,Cal: 120 kcal, Prt20 g, Fats: 3 g

4.58 Creamy Avocado Soup

Time for cook: 10 mins, **Complexity level:** easy, **Time for prep.:** 5 mins, **Portions:** 2

Ingredients

- 1 ripe avocado, peeled and pitted
- 1 cup vegetable broth
- 1/4 cup Greek yogurt
- 1 tbsp lime juice
- Salt and pepper to taste
- Chopped cilantro for garnish (optional)

Directions

1. Combine avocado, vegetable broth, Greek yogurt, and lime juice in a blender. Blend until smooth.
2. Season with salt and pepper to taste.
3. Transfer the soup to a saucepan and heat over medium heat until warm.
4. Garnish with chopped cilantro, if desired. Serve warm.

Nutritional information

Carbs: 8 g,Cal: 160 kcal, Prt6 g, Fats: 12 g

4.59 Creamy Tomato Soup

Time for cook: 15 mins, **Complexity level:** easy, **Time for prep.:** 5 mins, **Portions:** 2

Ingredients

- 1 cup tomato puree
- 1 cup vegetable broth
- 1/4 cup heavy cream
- Salt and pepper to taste
- Fresh basil for garnish (optional)

Directions

1. In a saucepan, combine tomato puree and vegetable broth. Heat over medium heat.
2. Stir in heavy cream and season with salt and pepper.
3. Cook for about 10 minutes, until heated through.
4. Garnish with fresh basil, if desired. Serve warm.

Nutritional information

Carbs: 9 g,Cal: 130 kcal, Prt2 g, Fats: 10 g

Chapter 5: Semisolid / Soft Foods

5.1 Sweet Potato Egg Casserole

Time for cook: 1 hr 10 mins, **Complexity level:** hard, **Time for prep.:** 15 mins, **Portions:** 1

Ingredients

- Sweet potatoes ½
- Pepper to taste
- Bunch asparagus ¼
- Yogurt 1/4 cup
- Bacon 1 slice
- Salt to taste
- Butter 1/2 tbsp
- Egg whites 1
- Egg 1
- Onion 1/2

Directions

1. Put the air fryer just on 400 ° F setting.
2. Heat the olive oil using an air fryer, then cook the bacon lasted for approximately six-ten mins, stirring it occasionally. Slices of cooked bacon should be removed and put aside.
3. Sweet potatoes should be diced, and asparagus should be laid in a basin. Add pepper, salt, and other components to the mixture before moving it to the air fryer. Cook for like twenty minutes, rotating as necessary and checking halfway through.
4. Place onions within melted butter and sauté over moderate flame until quite caramelized (browned). It takes roughly ten minutes.
5. Greek yogurt, egg yolks, and whites should all be combined on a separate plate. Blend everything up entirely with a whisk.
6. Combine the sweet potato plus asparagus mixture with the bacon and onion in a bowl. Pour the eggs in to mix, giving them a good toss to distribute evenly.
7. Cook for a predetermined period of 30 minutes. Before slicing, let the chilling process finish.

Nutritional information

Carbs: 32.6 g, Cal: 395 kcal, Prt: 22.2 g, Fats: 19.1 g

5.2 Apple Crumble Ramekins

Time for cook: 35 mins, **Complexity level:** medium, **Time for prep.:** 10-12 mins, **Portions:** 1

Ingredients

- Apples peeled 1
- Apple pie 1/8 of tsp (spice)
- Sweetener 1.50 tbsp (no-calorie)

Topping

- Cereal (High fiber) ¼ of cup
- Almonds (Sliced) 0.50 tbsp
- Butter 0.50 tbsp
- Sweetener 0.50 tbsp (No-calorie)

Directions

1. We heat our air fryer up to 325 F. Coat the basket with non-stick frying spray.
2. Combine pie spice, apples, and a sweetener; cook well for three minutes or till the apples seem soft. Place the mixture into ramekins.
3. To make the mixture, place the sweetener, cereal, butter, and almonds together in a food processor and pulse to just smooth. Pour your mixture evenly into each ramekin.
4. Set a timer for thirty-five minutes and cook until the filling is bubbling on top and the topping becomes crispy.

Nutritional information

Carbs: 41.5 g, Cal: 215 kcal, Prt: 2.4 g, Fats: 7.9 g

5.3 Chocolate Mint Protein Pots

Time for cook: 20 mins, **Complexity level:** easy, **Time for prep.:** 5 mins, **Portions:** 1

Ingredients

- Milk 1% 1/4 cup
- Mint extract 1 pinch
- Chocolate protein powder ½ scoop
- Large eggs ½
- No-calorie sweetener 1/2 tbsp
- Pure vanilla extract 1 drop
- Unsweetened cocoa powder 1/2 tbsp

Directions

1. Protein, milk, sugar, chocolate powder, and vanilla should all be blended. One more time, blend in the eggs.
2. Place the four ramekins in the air fryer. Equally, divide the ingredients among the four ramekins.
3. Pour enough boiling water into the fryer to cover the ramekins' edges halfway.
4. Cook for about 20 minutes at 325F in an air fryer that has been preheated. A crust like a brownie will almost immediately form on the top. When finished, they should jiggle slightly but not contain any liquid. The final texture will resemble fudge.

Nutritional information

Carbs: 10.2 g, Cal: 142 kcal, Prt: 16.4 g, Fats: 4.9 g

5.4 Salty Caramel Dessert

Time for cook: 15-17 mins, **Complexity level:** easy, **Time for prep.:** 5 mins, **Portions:** 1

Ingredients

- Pudding 3 oz
- Salt 1 pinch
- A pinch cinnamon
- Whipped topping 1 tbsp
- Caramel sauce1 tsp

Directions

1. Gently whisk all of the pudding's components together.
2. Cook the meal in an air fryer preheated to 180F for about 15 minutes.
3. Put the prepared pudding cup on the dessert plate of your choice. In a bowl, mix the salt and cinnamon.
4. Whipped cream and caramel sauce are added on top.

Nutritional information

Carbs: 77.5 g, Cal: 327 kcal, Prt: 0.1 g, Fats: 0.7 g

5.5 Buffalo Styled Meat Balls

Time for cook: 30 mins, **Complexity level:** medium, **Time for prep.:** 15-16 mins, **Portions:** 2

Ingredients

- Onion (diced) ½
- Buffalo wing sauce is 2 cups
- Textured vegetable protein is ½ cup
- Onion powder ¼ of tsp
- Green pepper (diced) is ½
- Salt to taste
- Chicken or turkey is 1 lb (ground)
- Ground black pepper is 1/4 tsp
- Blue cheese crumbles about 1/2 cup
- Garlic powder is ¼ tsp
- Unflavored Greek yogurt is 1/3 cup

Directions

1. Combine the meat, yogurt, cheese, Buffalo sauce, TVP, peppers, onion, and so on in a sizable bowl. Add salt and pepper to your liking.
2. Scoop out some of the meat mixtures, then form them into meatballs.
3. Air fry at 320F for approximately twenty to thirty minutes.

Nutritional information

Carbs: 10.1 g, Cal: 648 kcal, Prt: 102.2 g, Fats: 21.7 g

5.6 Cheese Stake Scramble

Time for cook: 15 mins, **Complexity level:** easy, **Time for prep.:** 5 mins, **Portions:** 1

Ingredients

- Roast beef (shredded) 2 oz.
- Cow cheese 1 oz
- Onion (chopped) 2 tbsp
- Large egg 1
- Green pepper (chopped) 2 tbsp

Directions

1. Finely chop and sauté onion. Green pepper is added and cooked for about three mins at 375 F.
2. Sauté the beef shreds lasted approximately ten minutes, preferably when they were crispy.
3. Put the egg into the pan and employ a spoon to turn it.
4. After placing it on top, fold the cheese out over the egg mix to distribute it evenly.
5. Put on a serving platter and top with the garnishes of your choice.

Nutritional information

Carbs: 4.1 g, Cal: 230 kcal, Prt: 25.1 g, Fats: 12 g

5.7 Corned Beef

Time for cook: 25 mins, Complexity level: easy, Time for prep.: 5 mins, Portions: 2

Ingredients

- Yellow squash, about 1 cup
- Corned beef (chopped) is 4 oz.
- Onion (diced) ½
- Fresh black pepper is 1 pinch
- Garlic, minced is 1 clove

Directions

1. Squash and onions should then be added. Once they have softened, add the garlic; cook it on an air fryer that has been warmed to 400F when it is aromatic.
2. Slice some beef.
3. Put it in the veggies, at the absolute least.
4. Cook the pork and vegetables for a further seven to ten mins, preferably when they get crispy.

Nutritional information

Carbs: 46.8 g, Cal: 773 kcal, Prt: 36.8 g, Fats: 48.1 g

5.8 Creamy Beef

Time for cook: 20 mins, **Complexity level**: easy, **Time for prep.:** 5 mins, **Portions:** 2

Ingredients

- Lean beef (ground) is 1lb
- Hot water is 2 cups
- Atkins baking mix is 4 tbsp
- Salt 1 tbsp
- Olive oil 1 tsp
- Onion powder is 1 tbsp
- Garlic powder is 1 tbsp

Directions

1. Add ground beef to the basket of the air-fryer halfway. Add salt, pepper, garlic powder, seasonings, and onion powder to the meat.
2. Mix the spices into the meat and crush it using a wooden spoon.
3. Fry the beef in the air fryer at 400 °F for five minutes. Cook for another three to five minutes, preferably until well done. Mash the whole thing with a wooden spoon. Remove when done. Use Atkins baking powder mixed with water to make a thick gravy during an air fryer. Now include the cooked meat.

Nutritional information

Carbs: 9.8 g, Cal: 507 kcal, Prt: 76.4 g, Fats: 16.8 g

5.9 Italian Melt Casserole

Time for cook: 35 mins, **Complexity level**: easy, **Time for prep.:** 5 mins, **Portions:** 1

Ingredients

- Vidalia onion is ½ (chopped)
- Shredded cheese is ½ of a cup (Italian Blend)
- Garlic 1/2 clove
- Tomatoes 5 oz
- Cannellini beans about 6 oz
- Baby spinach 1/2 of bag
- Ground turkey is ½ lb
- Sliced mushrooms are ¼ cup

Directions

1. When the air fryer has reached 350F, put the onion and spinach to cook until soft.
2. Mushrooms and garlic should be added immediately. One more minute of cooking is done.
3. Tomatoes and beans should be added to the pan, and the mixture should be cooked for several mins.
4. It should be put inside a baking dish with cheese on top, then baked for thirty min.

Nutritional information

Carbs: 10.1 g, Cal: 722 kcal, Prt: 62.6 g, Fats: 50.5 g

5.10 Lasagna Meatball

Time for cook: 1 hr, **Complexity level:** difficult, **Time for prep.:** 15-17 mins, **Portions:** 2

Ingredients

- Ground beef is 1/4 lb
- Turkey meatballs 2
- Water 1/4 cup
- Zucchini 1 (grilled, sliced)
- Shredded mozzarella is 1/4 cup
- Tvp 2 tbsp
- Light goat cheese is 2 oz
- Spaghetti sauce is 1/2 cup
- Pesto 1 tsp
- Yellow squash 1 (grilled, sliced)

Directions

1. Mix TVP and water together, then add ground beef, and TVP to an air fryer.
2. Put it on a dish for serving. Spread goat cheese with pesto over the top. Grilled zucchini and squash are layered on top.
3. Distribute the meatballs evenly and drizzle the spaghetti sauce on top.
4. Sprinkle mozzarella cheese over the dish, then bake in an air fryer for approximately thirty-forty-five minutes until bubbling and hot.

Nutritional information

Carbs: 27.5 g, Cal: 529 kcal, Prt: 50 g, Fats: 24 g

5.11 Pork Meatballs

Time for cook: 20 mins, **Complexity level:** easy, **Time for prep.:** 10-12 mins, **Portions:** 12

Ingredients

- Ground pork is 12 oz
- Paprika ½ tsp
- Ground Italian sausage is 8 oz
- Dried parsley is 1 tsp
- Breadcrumbs are ½ cup
- Salt 1 tsp
- Egg 1

Directions

1. Heat the air fryer at 350 °F; combine pork, salt, sausage, parsley, egg, breadcrumbs, and paprika; add all to the air fryer. Scoop out twelve meatballs of the same size from the meat. The meatballs should be placed above a baking sheet.
2. The cooking time is eight minutes; shaking the basket after cooking for two more minutes. Allow the serving dish to settle for five minutes.

Nutritional information

Carbs: 3.3 g, Cal: 128 kcal, Prt: 12.2 g, Fats: 7 g

5.12 Cheesy Chicken plus Broccoli

Time for cook: 30 mins, **Complexity level:** medium, **Time for prep.:** 15-17 mins, **Portions:** 1

Ingredients

- Chicken breast is 4 oz
- Cream (Chicken soup) is 4 oz
- Pepper (to taste)
- Cheese (Shredded) 0.50 cup
- Broccoli florets 0.50 cup (Frozen)
- Onion to taste (in powder)
- Salt (to taste)
- Garlic to taste (in powder)
- Cauliflower florets are one cup
- Grated cheese 1/4 cup (parmesan)

Directions

1. We only heat up an air fryer up to 400 F.
2. Coat the air fryer with olive oil, then cook the chicken for approximately ten minutes.
3. Cook the cauliflower and broccoli for eight to ten mins, then mash them. Add the chicken mix and the mashed cauliflower to the soup. Merge all the above.
4. Sprinkle both types of cheese on top, and cook for over thirty min, stopping the timer only when your preferred level of cheese is attained.

Nutritional information

Carbs: 17.4 g, Cal: 522 kcal, Prt: 46.3 g, Fats: 29.9 g

5.13 Curried Cabbage & Chicken

Time for cook: 30 mins, **Complexity level:** easy, **Time for prep.:** 10-12 mins, **Portions:** 2

Ingredients

- Green cabbage 1/2
- Pepper (red) flakes 1 pinch
- Chicken broth is 2 cups
- Garlic ½ tbsp (powder)
- Salt to taste
- Curry (powder) is one tbsp
- Pepper to taste
- Frozen peas ½ cup
- Chicken breast ½ lb
- Onion 1/2
- Red potato 1

Directions

1. We only set an air fryer's temperature up to 375 F.
2. Fry potatoes, cabbage, and chicken broth since the vegetables are fork-tender and soft.
3. You may now begin boiling your peas, onion, chicken, and seasonings. Set the timer for fifteen min and cook since the veggies are tender and the liquid has been substantially reduced.
4. Serve warm.

Nutritional information

Carbs: 39 g, Cal: 423 kcal, Prt: 50 g, Fats: 7.6 g

5.14 Curried Chicken with Rice

Time for cook: 23 mins, **Complexity level:** easy, **Time for prep.:** 30 mins, **Portions:** 2

Ingredients

- Onion 1
- Pepper (taste-wise)
- Cauliflower rice is one batch
- Curry (powder) one tbsp
- veggies 12 oz (Mixed)
- Salt (taste-wise)
- Masala (garam) ½ of tsp
- Corn-starch /flour is 2 tbsp
- Chicken piece (any) one lb
- Clove garlic 1
- Cayenne pepper dash
- Coldwater 2 tbsp
- Water 1/2 cup

Directions

1. Take one bowl, and fill it with veggies, a piece of chicken, and a mixture of spices (cayenne, salt, curry powder, pepper, and chopped garlic).
2. Once the chicken has just been seasoned on all sides, combine everything. Leave to marinate for thirty min, covered.
3. We simply heat up an air fryer up to 400 F.
4. Add the chicken and simmer over fifteen min.
5. When your chicken reaches an internal temperature of 165 degrees Fahrenheit, flip it over and cook it for another eight minutes.
6. Put some cooked cauliflower rice on the side.

Nutritional information

Carbs: 25.3 g, Cal: 221 kcal, Prt: 17.7 g, Fats: 5.6 g

5.15 Enchiladas

Time for cook: 15 mins, **Complexity level:** easy, **Time for prep.:** 5 mins, **Portions:** 2

Ingredients

- Tortillas, wheat 6
- White onion ½
- Cooking spray as per need
- Sauce(enchilada) ½ of can
- Green pepper ½
- Minced garlic is one tsp
- Pepper flakes ¼ of tsp (red)
- Mexican blend cheese, about one cup
- Chicken breasts 2

Directions

1. Slicing up a chicken breast and putting it all in a single bowl.
2. Finely chop the onions and put the peppers and red pepper flakes.
3. Line your air fryer's basket with aluminum foil.
4. Arrange your tortillas into a casserole dish, top it up, and add enchilada sauce.
5. Spread some cheese and additional enchilada sauce over the top of a chicken and onion that you've placed in the center of the tortillas.
6. Roll your tortillas with care, then arrange them inside your fryer. The enchiladas should be topped with more sauce and cheese.
7. For this recipe, we set the air fryer to 325 °F & cook for fifteen min.

Nutritional information

Carbs: 48.4 g, Cal: 362 kcal, Prt: 32.8 g, Fats: 8.3 g

5.16 Gobble Down Pizza

Time for cook: 20-25 mins, **Complexity level:** easy, **Time for prep.:** 8 mins, **Portions:** 2

Ingredients

- Flatbread thins 2
- Mayonnaise one tbsp
- Cranberry Sauce is 2 tbsp
- Stuffing one oz (leftover)
- Turkey (Roast) is 2 oz
- Cheese (Cheddar) ¼ of cup

Directions

1. We just heat up an air fryer up to 325 F.
2. Place the flatbreads upon the nonstick sheet side by side and space them apart by a few inches.
3. Mayo and cranberry sauce should be combined in one bowl. Place equally half of the mix onto each flatbread.
4. Evenly distribute the turkey meat well over the sauce. The filling should then be formed into little circles using just a tiny scoop.
5. Now, evenly distribute cheese over the ingredients of your pizza. Start a timer for eight to ten minutes and heat until the cheese melts.
6. Let the pizza cool a little before slicing and serving.

Nutritional information

Carbs: 20.7 g, Cal: 222 kcal, Prt: 8.1 g, Fats: 12.1 g

5.17 Protein-y Zuccini Fritters

Time for cook: 10 mins, **Complexity level:** easy, **Time for prep.:** 5 mins, **Portions:** 2

Ingredients

- Zucchini grated ¼
- Old bay seasoning (pinch)
- Tvp 48g
- Herbs de Provence about ¼ of tsp
- Mayo 1/4 tbsp
- Dijon mustard (Pinch)
- Pinch of salt
- Garlic, minced ¼

Directions

1. We only heat up an air fryer up to 400 F.
2. Coat an air fryer with some olive oil by swirling it.
3. Shred your zucchini, season it with salt and pepper, and set it aside for five minutes to allow the water to drain.
4. Mix TVP. Add herbs along with mayo, TVP, and mustard. Before creating patties, wait five minutes.
5. For each face, use a timer to cook them in the fryer for four to five minutes.

Nutritional information

Carbs: 9.8 g, Cal: 102 kcal, Prt: 11.3 g, Fats: 2.8 g

5.18 Queso Chicken

Time for cook: 40 mins, **Complexity level:** easy, **Time for prep.:** 10 mins, **Portions:** 1

Ingredients

- Chicken (breasts) ¼ of lb.
- Salsa 1/4 jar
- Olive oil ¼ of tsp
- Cheese soup is ½ cup
- Beans (Black)1/4 of an

Directions

1. We only heat up an air fryer up to 400 F.
2. Coat an air fryer with a layer of olive oil; now, cover the chicken with salsa, and cook for seven to ten minutes.
3. Once the beans have been drained and combined with the cheese soup, continue cooking for thirty minutes while stirring occasionally.
4. Cook for a maximum of thirty more minutes while stirring periodically.

Nutritional information

Carbs: 37.5 g, Cal: 467 kcal, Prt: 46.5 g, Fats: 14.4 g

5.19 Bacon-Wrapped Avocado

Time for cook: 15 mins, **Complexity level:** easy, **Time for prep.:** 15-20 mins, **Portions:** 2

Ingredients

- Bacon strips 6
- Avocados 2

Sauce

- Mayonnaise ¼ cup
- Lime juice is one tbsp
- Chili sauce (Sriracha) is 1 -1.5 tbsp
- Lime zest (Grated) is ½ tsp

Directions

1. We only heat up an air fryer up to 400F. The basket should be coated with nonstick frying spray.
2. Divide the Avocado in half, then into thirds for each half. One bacon strip is folded into one wedge.
3. Arrange the wedges so that they are in one layer in the basket of an air fryer. Ten to fifteen minutes should be spent cooking.
4. Mix the items for the sauce in the bowl before serving it with wedges.

Nutritional information

Carbs: 17.4 g, Cal: 627 kcal, Prt: 14.2 g, Fats: 56.4 g

5.20 Eggplant Parmesan Casserole

Time for cook: 35-40 mins, **Complexity level:** medium, **Time for prep.:** 5 mins, **Portions:** 1

Ingredients

- Eggplant 0.25
- Tomatoes 1/8 cup
- Alfredo sauce 0.25
- Spaghetti squash 0.50 cup.
- Green pepper 0.25
- Onion 0.25
- Cheese 0.38 cup.

Directions

1. We simply heat up an air fryer up to 325 F.
2. Use oil to coat the green pepper, onions, and eggplant; add pepper, salt, and Italian seasoning; and roast for at minimum twenty-five minutes.
3. Put the tomatoes, roasted veggies, and spaghetti squash in one bowl. Add seasoning once more to your meal to give it flavor.
4. Distribute some cheese up on top, then cook over another almost twenty minutes when the cheese is well melted, chestnut brown in color.

Nutritional information

Carbs: 16.9 g, Cal: 252 kcal, Prt: 13.4 g, Fats: 15.5 g

5.21 Farmer's Market Scramble

Time for cook: 15 mins, **Complexity level:** easy, **Time for prep.:** 5 mins, **Portions:** 2

Ingredients

- Large onion ½
- Garlic 1 clove
- Pepper to taste
- Seasoning (Italian) is 1/4 tsp
- Cheese 2 oz
- Green pepper ½
- Yellow squash ¼
- Salt to taste
- Eggs 2
- Tomato cut 1
- Small zucchini ¼
- Red pepper ½

Directions

1. We prep up an air fryer up to 325 F.
2. Spray oil there in the fryer's basket and sauté vegetables and garlic. At this point, you may also add Italian seasoning.
3. Fill the crevices in the veggies with eggs, then cook them.
4. Spread cheese over it and turn the heat off.
5. Finish by adding fresh tomatoes.

Nutritional information

Carbs: 10.2 g, Cal: 222 kcal, Prt: 14.4 g, Fats: 14.2 g

5.22 Patty Pan Squash

Time for cook: 15 mins, **Complexity level:** easy, **Time for prep.:** 8-10 mins, **Portions:** 2

Ingredients

- Squash (pattypan) is 2.5 cups
- Oregano (Dried) is 1/8 tsp
- Thyme (Dried) is 1/8 tsp
- Salt ¼ tsp
- Pepper 1/8 tsp
- Parsley (Minced fresh) is ½ tbsp.
- Olive oil is ½ tbsp.
- Garlic clove 1

Directions

1. We only set up an air fryer's temperature to 375 F.
2. Combine the squash in a bowl along with the oil, thyme, pepper, garlic, salt, and oregano.
3. Place the squash in a layer there in a frying air basket on the greased baking sheet; cook for about 10-fifteen min.
4. Remove it from the basket and garnish it with parsley.

Nutritional information

Carbs: 11.7 g, Cal: 84 kcal, Prt: 2.5 g, Fats: 4.3 g

5.23 Bacon-Wrapped Shrimp

Time for cook: 10 mins, **Complexity level:** easy, **Time for prep.:** 10-12 mins, **Portions:** 2

Ingredients

- Thinly sliced bacon is 4 strips
- Jumbo Shrimp 8
- Steak seasoning is ½ tsp

Directions

1. Stir the steak spice into a bowl and add the shrimp to coat.
2. Half a piece of bacon should encircle each shrimp. Place inside a hot air fryer.
3. At 400 F, just let that air fry for approximately five min. Cook for an extra five mins after flipping.

Nutritional information

Carbs: 0 g, Cal: 360 kcal, Prt: 48 g, Fats: 18 g

5.24 Cajun Salmon

Time for cook: 10 mins, **Complexity level:** easy, **Time for prep.:** 10-12 mins, **Portions:** 2

Ingredients

- Salmon fillets about (skin on) 2
- Brown sugar is 1 tsp
- Cajun seasoning is 1 tbsp
- Cooking spray

Directions

1. Salmon fillets should be washed and dried. Apply cooking spray on them.
2. Spread the cajun seasoning and brown sugar together on a serving platter. By pressing these into the seasoning, the fillets are seasoned. The salmon fillets should be put inside the fryer's basket after being sprayed with cooking spray.
3. At 400F, air fried lasted approximately eight minutes on one side and two mins on the other.

Nutritional information

Carbs: 12.3 g, Cal: 280 kcal, Prt: 1.5 g, Fats: 41.1 g

5.25 Thai Peanut Sauce alongside Shrimp

Time for cook: 5 mins, **Complexity level:** easy, **Time for prep.:** 5 mins, **Portions:** 2

Ingredients

- Diced shrimp of about 3 oz
- Sesame seeds around 1 tsp
- Peanut Thai sauce is 2 tbsp
- Pine nuts are 1 tbsp
- An avocado (diced) is 1/4
- Honey 1 tbsp
- Craisins 2 tbsp
- Fish taco seasoning is 1 tbsp

Directions

1. Season the shrimp.
2. For about five minutes, air-fried shrimp at 400°F together in a prep air fryer.
3. Add some honey.
4. Combine the avocado, shrimp, craisins, and pine nuts in a mixing dish. Slowly drizzle in your peanut sauce. Sesame seeds ought to be put on top.

Nutritional information

Carbs: 22.4 g, Cal: 196 kcal, Prt: 11.6 g, Fats: 6.6 g

5.26 Lemon Pepper Shrimp

Time for cook: 10 mins, **Complexity level:** easy, **Time for prep.:** 5-6 mins, **Portions:** 2

Ingredients

- Olive oil is 1 tbsp
- Shrimp (uncooked) is 12 oz
- Lemon juiced 1
- Paprika ¼ tsp
- Lemon pepper is 1 tsp
- Lemon, sliced 1
- Garlic powder is ¼ tsp

Directions

1. Add the olive oil, garlic, paprika, lemon, and lemon pepper.
2. Completely cover the shrimp there in the mixture.
3. Cook the shrimp over six-eight minutes in an air fryer prep up to 400 ° F.
4. Serve with lemon.

Nutritional information

Carbs: 4.2 g, Cal: 240 kcal, Prt: 37.2 g, Fats: 9.4 g

5.27 Shrimp and Quinoa

Time for cook: 35 mins, **Complexity level:** medium, **Time for prep.:** 5 mins, **Portions:** 1

Ingredients

- Bacon 1/4 cup
- Shrimp 2
- Cloves garlic 2
- Quinoa 3/4 cup
- Onion 1
- Chives 1 tablespoon
- Tomatoes 1
- Water 1 1/2 cups
- Yogurt 2 tbsp.
- Salt 1/4 tsp.
- Green bell pepper is ½
- Hot sauce 1/2 tsp.
- Dry white wine is 1/4 cup.

Directions

1. Prepare the bacon by placing it into an air fryer that has been prep up to 400 °F for seven–10 minutes. Vegetables are air fried for around eight minutes. When the bacon has finished cooking, put it on a plate.
2. Cook the veggies for approximately eight minutes, occasionally stirring, just when they are soft.
3. Bring the wine, salt, tomatoes, yogurt, and spicy sauce to a boil while occasionally scraping the browned pieces off the fryer's bottom. To mix the flavors and thicken the sauce, cook for approximately six to eight minutes at 350F. Add the bacon back to the pan. Cook for another one–2 minutes.

   Nutritional information

Carbs: 101 g, Cal: 746 kcal, Prt: 47.8 g, Fats: 11.8 g

5.28 Furikake Salmon

Time for cook: 10 mins, **Complexity level:** easy, **Time for prep.:** 5 mins, **Portions:** 3

Ingredients

- Mayonnaise 1/2 cup
- Furikake 2 tbsp
- Pepper to taste
- Salmon fillet is 1 pound
- Salt to taste
- Shoyu 1 tbsp

Directions

1. We put 400 F to prepare an air fryer.
2. In a bowl, mix shoyu and mayonnaise. After completely combining, put it away.
3. Apply paper towels to the salmon fillet to dry it. Use salt and pepper to season the fillet on both sides. Lay the meat skin side down if you prefer to cook it with its skin on.
4. Spread the salmon with an equal layer of the mayonnaise-shoyu mixture. Mayonnaise is topped over furikake.
5. Use a nonstick spray to coat the fryer basket. Facing the skin down, place the salmon fillet.
6. **Nutritional information**

Carbs: 1o.6 g, Cal: 360 kcal, Prt: 30 g, Fats: 22.4 g

5.29 Salmon Nuggets

Time for cook: 15 mins, **Complexity level:** easy, **Time for prep.:** 20-22 mins, **Portions:** 4

Ingredients

- Maple syrup is 1/4 cup
- Skinless salmon fillet of about ½ lb
- The dried chipotle pepper is (ground) 1 pinch
- Cooking spray
- Sea salt ½ pinch
- Croutons around ¾ cup (Butter garlic-flavor)
- Large egg 1/2

Directions

1. Bring the chipotle powder, salt, and maple syrup to a boil in one pot.
2. Mash the egg together in a mixing bowl.
3. Croutons should be ground into crumbs in a food processor before being placed in a bowl. Salmon should be dipped in egg mix first, then crouton crumbs.
4. We prep an air fryer up to 400F and cook this coated fish lasting three minutes. Allow it to cook for about three mins on the opposite side.
5. Remove them from the oven and pour maple syrup on top before serving.

Nutritional information

Carbs: 22.7 g, Cal: 178 kcal, Prt: 11.2 g, Fats: 5.1 g

5.30 Lemon vinaigrette dressing

Time for cook: 0 mins, **Complexity level:** easy, **Time for prep.:** 5 mins, **Portions:** 8

Ingredients

- Lemon juice, about 1/3 cup
- Olive oil 1/3 cup
- Sea salt about 1/4 tsp
- Lemon peel about 1 tsp (shredded)
- Fresh garlic, about 4 cloves

Directions

1. All components should be combined in a clean bowl and whisked together.
2. Serve with vegetables and fresh spinach for a flavorful side salad.

Nutritional information

Carbs: 1 g, Cal: 77 kcal, Prt: 0 g, Fats: 8 g

5.31 Magic Green Sauce

Time for cook: 0 mins, **Complexity level:** easy, **Time for prep.:** 5 mins, **Portions:** 8

Ingredients

- Avocado 1
- Salt 1 tsp
- Pistachios 1/2 cup
- Olive oil 1/2 cup
- Parsley, cilantro leaves 1 cup (combined)
- Water 1/2 cup
- Jalapeno 1
- Juice of lime 1
- Garlic 2 cloves

Directions

1. All ingredients, excluding the pistachios, should be processed in a food processor until combined.
2. Pistachios are added and processed till nearly smooth.
3. Use it as a sauce, spread, or dip.

Nutritional information

Carbs: 5.4 g, Cal: 199 kcal, Prt: 2.3 g, Fats: 20.2 g

5.32 Caesar Dressing (Low-Fat)

Time for cook: 0 mins, **Complexity level:** easy, **Time for prep.:** 10 mins, **Portions:** 1

Ingredients

- Lemon juice is ¼ cup
- Black pepper is ½ tsp
- Milk is ¼ cup (low-fat)
- Onion powder is 1 tsp
- Olive oil is 1 tbsp
- Minced garlic is 1 tsp
- Dijon mustard is 1 tsp
- anchovy fillets 2
- Worcestershire sauce is 2 tsp

Directions

1. Mix the yogurt, onion powder, cheese, mustard, lemon juice, garlic, milk, Worcestershire sauce, olive oil, pepper, and anchovies on high speed in a blender till the mixture is creamy and smooth with no lumps.

Nutritional information

Carbs: 2 g, Cal: 48 kcal, Prt: 4 g, Fats: 4 g

5.33 Ruby French Dressing

Time for cook: 0 mins, **Complexity level:** easy, **Time for prep.:** 5 mins, **Portions:** 1

Ingredients

- Olive oil is 1/2 cup
- Black pepper ½ tsp
- Ketchup 1/3 cup
- Lemon juice is 2 tsp
- Sea salt ½ tsp
- Splenda 1/4 cup/ truvia 3 tbsp
- Paprika 1 tsp
- White vinegar 1/4 cup
- Dry mustard 1 tsp
- Chopped onion 1 tbsp

Directions

1. Blend the following ingredients in a blender: oil, pepper, ketchup, salt sweetener, paprika, vinegar, mustard, onion, and lemon juice. Cover and process until smooth.
2. Keep these in the fridge together in a mason jar. Shake well before using.

Nutritional information

Carbs: 2 g, Cal: 27 kcal, Prt: 0 g, Fats: 0 g

5.34 Autumn Egg White Omelet

Time for cook: 10 minutes, **Complexity level:** easy, **Time for prep.:** 10 minutes, **Portions:** 2

Ingredients

- ⅛ cup of diced mushrooms
- 4 to 5 grape tomatoes, halved
- Half apple, chopped
- ⅛ cup of diced onion
- ¼ cup of broccoli florets
- 2 cups of baby spinach, fresh
- ⅛ cup of diced bell pepper
- Half a cup of egg whites
- Sea salt & black pepper
- Cinnamon, a pinch

Directions

1. Sauté the mushroom & onion in a splash of oil for 3-5 minutes.
2. Add broccoli, bell pepper & apple to the pan, and cook for 1 to 2 minutes.
3. Add the seasonings with spinach, and cook for a few minutes.
4. Add tomatoes, and cook for a few minutes. Take it out on a plate.
5. Add the egg whites, coat the whole pan, and add the vegetable mixture to one-half of the eggs as it sets.
6. Place the other half on top. Serve warm.

Nutritional information

Carbs: 25 g, Cal: 189 kcal, Prt: 19 g, Fats: 1 g

5.35 Lean Turkey Chili

Time for cook: 50 minutes, **Complexity level:** Medium, **Time for prep.:** 10 minutes, **Portions:** 4-6

Ingredients

- 1 tbsp. of olive oil
- 1 cup of chicken broth
- 1 can of black beans
- 1/4 onion, diced
- 1 lb. of lean ground turkey
- 1 can of (28 oz.) crushed tomatoes
- 1 tsp. of cumin
- 1 can of kidney beans, rinsed
- 2 tbsp. of chili powder
- Salt & pepper, to taste

Directions

1. Saute onion in hot oil until translucent & take it out on a plate.
2. Add turkey to the pan, and cook until done.
3. Add the rest of the ingredients with the onion, and mix well.
4. Cook for 40 minutes on low, covered.
5. Serve after adjusting seasoning.

Nutritional information

Carbs: 21 g, Cal: 390 kcal, Prt: 12 g, Fats: 10 g

5.36 Pan-Seared Tilapia

Time for cook: 7 minutes, **Complexity level:** easy, **Time for prep.:** 10 minutes, **Portions:** 1

Ingredients

- Half tbsp. of seafood seasoning
- 2 oz. of tilapia fillet

Directions

1. Season the fish with seafood seasoning.
2. Oil spray a pan & place on medium flame.
3. Add the seasoned fish & cook for 7 minutes until flaky.

Nutritional information

Carbs: 1 g, Cal: 61 kcal, Prt: 12 g, Fats: 1 g

5.37 Crockpot Chicken Curry

Time for cook: 4-8 hours, **Complexity level:** medium, **Time for prep.:** 20 minutes, **Portions:** 4

Ingredients

- 5 Garlic Cloves
- 1 tsp. of grated ginger
- 2 tsp. of Ground Turmeric
- 2 Tomatoes
- 1 Onion
- 24 oz. of Chicken
- 1 tbsp. of Whole Cloves
- 6 oz. of Baby Spinach

- 1 tsp. of Salt
- Half tsp. of Cayenne Pepper
- 1 tsp. of Cinnamon
- 1 tsp. of Garam Masala
- Half a cup of Yogurt

- 4 Cardamom Pods

Directions

1. Add everything except for whole spices, chicken & spinach to a food processor.
2. Pulse until smooth.
3. Add chicken & whole spices to the crockpot, and add the blended sauce.
4. Cook for 7 hours on low or on high for 3 hours.
5. Add spinach & cook for 1 more hour.
6. Shred the chicken & serve.

Nutritional information

Carbs: 8 g, Cal: 186 kcal, Prt: 28 g, Fats: 4 g

5.38 Pan Fried Trout Fillet

Time for cook: 15 minutes, **Complexity level:** easy, **Time for prep.:** 10 minutes, **Portions:** 3

Ingredients

- 1 tsp. of Salt
- Half tsp. of Black Pepper
- 1 Onion, sliced
- 1 tbsp. of Italian Seasoning

- 3 Trout Fillet
- 1 tbsp. of Olive Oil
- 1 tbsp. of Butter

Directions

1. Wash & pat dry the fish.
2. Season with the seasonings.
3. Add butter & oil to a pan. Add onion & sauté until translucent.
4. Add the fish to the onion, skin side down. Cook for 3 minutes on medium flame.
5. Flip & cook for 3 minutes more. Serve warm.

Nutritional information

Carbs: 5 g, Cal: 91 kcal, Prt: 21 g, Fats: 6 g

5.39 Deviled Egg & Bacon

Time for cook: 0 minutes, **Complexity level:** easy, **Time for prep.:** 20 minutes, **Portions:** 8

Ingredients

- 3 tbsp. of canned chickpeas, rinsed
- ¼ tsp. of Paprika
- 2 tbsp. of chopped Dill
- Half a cup of yogurt

- 8 hardboiled Eggs, peeled
- 1 tbsp. of Dijon mustard
- 2 Slices of cooked bacon, crumbled

Directions

1. Slice eggs in half, lengthwise. Take the yolks out.
2. Only use 4 of the yolks, and add to a food processor.
3. Add the rest of the ingredients. Pulse until smooth.
4. Add this mixture to egg whites, and serve.

Nutritional information

Carbs: 2.5 g, Cal: 77 kcal, Prt: 8 g, Fats: 3 g

5.40 Mexican Breakfast Casserole

Time for cook: 30 minutes, **Complexity level:** easy, **Time for prep.:** 20 minutes, **Portions:** 8

Ingredients

- 1 tomato, chopped
- 1 tsp. of mustard powder
- 4 oz. of canned diced green chilies
- 2 tbsp. of heavy cream
- 8 eggs
- 1 tsp. of baking powder
- 1 oz. of cheddar cheese shredded
- Salt, a pinch
- 2 oz. of diced red onion

Directions

1. Let the oven preheat to 350 F.
2. In a bowl, add all ingredients & whisk well.
3. Add to an oil-sprayed pan, bake for half an hour.
4. Slice & serve.

Nutritional information

Carbs: 6 g, Cal: 89 kcal, Prt: 12 g, Fats: 8 g

5.41 Oven-Baked Salmon

Time for cook: 15 minutes, **Complexity level:** easy, **Time for prep.:** 20 minutes, **Portions:** 4

Ingredients

- 1 tbsp. of olive oil
- 2 garlic cloves, chopped
- Black pepper, to taste
- 1 tbsp. of lemon juice
- 1-pound of salmon filet
- Half tsp. of each dill, basil, parsley & thyme
- 1/4 tsp. of salt
- 1 pat of butter

Directions

1. Let the oven preheat to 400 F.
2. Oil spray a large piece of foil. Add fish fillets side by side.
3. Add one tbsp. oil & one tbsp. of lemon juice on fish fillet & rub them all over.
4. Add the herbs, salt & pepper. Place pats on butter on top.
5. Close the foil.
6. Bake for 12 to 15 minutes. Serve.

Nutritional information

Carbs: 6 g, Cal: 78 kcal, Prt: 21 g, Fats: 7 g

5.42 Italian Poached Eggs

Time for cook: 12 minutes, **Complexity level:** medium, **Time for prep.:** 10 minutes, **Portions:** 4

Ingredients

- Salt and pepper, to taste
- 3 to 4 roasted jarred red pepper, sliced
- 4 eggs
- 16 oz. of Marinara Sauce
- 4 fresh basil leaves, torn

Directions

1. Add red peppers & sauce to a pan on medium flame.
2. Heat it well & crack eggs after making an indentation. Add salt & pepper.
3. Cook for 12 minutes with a lid on top.
4. Turn the heat off, and serve with fresh basil on top.

Nutritional information

Carbs: 4 g, Cal: 114 kcal, Prt: 8 g, Fats: 6 g

5.43 Black Bean Burger

Time for cook: 12 minutes, **Complexity level:** medium, **Time for prep.:** 10 minutes, **Portions:** 4

Ingredients

- ¼ cup of Chopped Carrots
- ¼ cup of Parsley
- 1 tsp. of Onion Powder
- Half tsp. of Black Pepper
- 2 cups of canned Black beans
- Half of a Sweet Red Pepper
- Half a cup of Breadcrumbs
- 3 tsp. of Dijon Mustard
- 1 tsp. of Chili Powder
- Half tsp. of Sea Salt
- 1/3 tsp. of Garlic Powder

Directions

1. Sauté the carrots, & onion for 2 minutes in hot oil.
2. Add onion powder, chili & garlic, and cook for a few minutes.
3. Add the mixture to a food processor with parsley. Pulse many times, then add beans & pulse 5-6 times. Do not over-mix.
4. Transfer to a bowl with pepper, breadcrumbs, salt & mustard.
5. Mix & make into 4 patties. Oil spray a pan & cook patties for 7 to 8 minutes.
6. Serve.

Nutritional information

Carbs: 33 g, Cal: 186 kcal, Prt: 10 g, Fats: 1 g

5.44 Pork Taco Soup

Time for cook: 30 minutes, **Complexity level:** medium, **Time for prep.:** 10 minutes, **Portions:** 4

Ingredients

- ¼ tsp. of Paprika
- ¼ lb. of Lean ground pork
- Half tbsp. of Olive oil
- ¼ tsp. of Garlic powder
- Half tsp. of Cumin
- Half a cup of chopped Zucchini
- ¼ tsp. of Onion powder
- ⅛ tsp. of Dried oregano
- ¼ cup of canned black beans
- ⅛ cup of yogurt
- ¼ cup of canned pinto beans
- Half a cup of chicken broth
- ⅛ cup of chopped Cilantro

Directions

1. Add oregano, cumin, onion, paprika & garlic powder in a pan. Toast for 2 to 3 minutes.
2. Turn the heat to medium flame, add oil & cook for 1 minute.
3. Add pork & cook for 5 to 7 minutes.
4. Add broth, beans, pinto beans & zucchini, mix & boil.
5. Simmer on low flame for 4 to 5 minutes.
6. Serve with yogurt & cilantro on top.

Nutritional information

Carbs: 8.3 g, Cal: 99.4 kcal, Prt: 10 g, Fats: 3.3 g

5.45 Roasted Carrot Ginger Soup

Time for cook: 35 minutes, **Complexity level:** medium, **Time for prep.:** 15 minutes, **Portions:** 4

Ingredients

- 1 tbsp. of coconut oil
- Half yellow onion, cut into fours
- Half tbsp. of garam masala
- 1 can of (14 oz.) coconut milk
- 1 pound of carrots, sliced into coins
- Half tsp. of ground ginger
- 3 cups of vegetable broth
- 5 cloves of unpeeled garlic
- 1 lime's juice
- 3/4 tsp. of sea salt

Directions

1. Let the oven preheat to 425 F.
2. Spread the onion & carrots on a foil-lined baking sheet. Toss with garam masala & olive oil.
3. Season with salt & pepper. Add garlic with the carrots.
4. Meanwhile, heat the broth.
5. Roast the vegetables for 30-35 minutes, stirring after half time, until vegetables are tender.
6. Transfer to the blender with the rest of the ingredients. Pulse until smooth.
7. Adjust seasoning & serve.

Nutritional information

Carbs: 12 g, Cal: 108 kcal, Prt: 8 g, Fats: 7 g

5.46 Turkey Kale Meatballs

Time for cook: 35 minutes, **Complexity level:** medium, **Time for prep.:** 15 minutes, **Portions:** 5

Ingredients

- 1 ½ cups of Baby kale, chopped
- 1 tsp. of Garlic powder
- 1 tbsp. of Parmesan cheese
- 1 Egg
- 1 lb. of Lean ground turkey
- 2 tbsp. of chopped Parsley
- ¼ cup of yogurt
- 1 tsp. of Apple cider vinegar
- 2 tbsp. of chopped Dill

Directions

1. Let the oven preheat to 350 F.
2. Add egg, turkey, parmesan & kale. Mix well & make 16 meatballs.
3. Place on an oil-sprayed baking sheet. Bake for 25 to 30 minutes, flipping after halftime.
4. Add the rest of the ingredients to a bowl with one tbsp. of hot water. Mix well.
5. Serve the turkey meatballs with the sauce.

Nutritional information

Carbs: 1.6 g, Cal: 172 kcal, Prt: 32 g, Fats: 4.2 g

5.47 Crustless Pizza Casserole

Time for cook: 30 minutes, **Complexity level:** medium, **Time for prep.:** 15 minutes, **Portions:** 4

Ingredients

- 1 clove of garlic, minced
- 1 1/2 cups of pizza sauce
- 1 lb. of ground meat
- 2 cups of mixed diced vegetables
- Salt & pepper, to taste
- Pizza toppings, as needed

Directions

1. Let the oven preheat to 350 F.
2. Oil spray a skillet & sauté vegetables for 2-3 minutes.
3. Add garlic & cook for 1 minute.
4. Add meat & cook until done; drain any liquid.
5. Add sauce & mix well. Simmer for 5 to 7 minutes.
6. Transfer to a casserole dish & spread it evenly. Add toppings with cheese.
7. Bake for 20 minutes. Serve.

Nutritional information

Carbs: 11 g, Cal: 278 kcal, Prt: 21 g, Fats: 10 g

5.48 Barbecue Salmon

Time for cook: 10 minutes, **Complexity level:** easy, **Time for prep.:** 10 minutes, **Portions:** 4

Ingredients

- 4 tbsp. of bbq sauce (low sugar)
- 4 Salmon fillets each of 4 oz.
- 2 tbsp. of grill seasoning

Directions

1. Brush the thawed & patted dry fish fillet with BBQ sauce.
2. Add fish to preheated pan & cook for 5 minutes.
3. Add seasoning on top, flip & brush with BBQ sauce & add seasoning.
4. Cook for 1-2 minutes. Serve.

Nutritional information

Carbs: 7 g, Cal: 124 kcal, Prt: 22 g, Fats: 1 g

5.49 Curried Lentil Soup

Time for cook: 25 minutes, **Complexity level:** easy, **Time for prep.:** 10 minutes, **Portions:** 4

Ingredients

- 1 cup of chopped onion
- 1/8 tsp. of cayenne pepper
- 1 tbsp. of minced garlic
- 16 oz. of steamed lentils
- 1 tbsp. of minced ginger
- 1 tsp. of canola oil
- 1/4 tsp. of each black pepper & salt
- 1 1/2 tbsp. of curry powder
- 3 cups of vegetable broth
- 1/4 cup of yogurt
- 1 ½ tbsp. of balsamic vinegar
- 2 cups of fresh baby spinach
- 1/4 cup of cilantro

Directions

1. Sauté the onion in hot oil for 3 minutes.
2. Add ginger, garlic & cook for 1 minute.
3. Add curry & cayenne, and cook for half a minute.
4. Add lentils, vinegar & broth. Turn the heat to high & boil.
5. Simmer on low flame for 5 minutes.
6. Puree the soup with a stick blender.
7. Add salt, pepper & spinach, and cook until it wilts.
8. Serve with adding cilantro & yogurt on top.

Nutritional information

Carbs: 35 g, Cal: 210 kcal, Prt: 14 g, Fats: 2 g

5.50 Instant Pot Cauliflower Salad

Time for cook: 10 minutes, **Complexity level:** easy, **Time for prep.:** 10 minutes, **Portions:** 4

Ingredients

- 1 cup of water
- 4 hard-boiled eggs
- 1 tbsp. of yellow mustard
- 1 1/2 cups of yogurt
- 1 head of cauliflower
- 1 tbsp. of vinegar
- 2 stalks of celery
- 1 tsp. of salt
- 1/4 tsp. of black pepper
- Half onion

Directions

1. Break the cauliflower into small florets.
2. Add to an instant pot with water.
3. Seal & set for 5 minutes on the manual. Do the quick release.
4. Drain & transfer to a bowl.
5. Add the eggs after chopping them & mix with cauliflower.
6. Add the diced vegetables & other ingredients, mix with a fork & mash to a desired texture.

Nutritional information

Carbs: 3 g, Cal: 209 kcal, Prt: 9 g, Fats: 19 g

5.51 Cream Of Mushroom Chicken Thighs

Time for cook: 20 minutes, **Complexity level:** easy, **Time for prep.:** 10 minutes, **Portions:** 4-6

Ingredients

- 1 can of (10 oz.) no-fat cream of mushroom soup
- 1 lb. of chicken thighs, boneless & skinless

Directions

1. Let the oven preheat to 350F.
2. Trim the fat off of the chicken thighs & season generously with salt & pepper.
3. Add to a casserole dish, add a soup can & coat well.
4. Bake for 20 minutes.
5. Serve.

Nutritional information

Carbs: 4 g, Cal: 114 kcal, Prt: 16 g, Fats: 4 g

5.52 Chicken and Bean Bake

Time for cook: 45-60 minutes, **Complexity level:** easy, **Time for prep.:** 10 minutes, **Portions:** 4

Ingredients

- 1 cup of green beans
- 2 tsp. of chopped fresh herbs
- 6 chicken breasts, skinless
- Half tsp. of each salt & black pepper
- 1 to 2 tbsp. of olive oil
- 1 tsp. of minced garlic
- 2 cans of beans
- Red pepper flakes, to taste

Directions

1. In a casserole dish, add all ingredients except for chicken. Mix & add chicken on top.
2. Drizzle oil on top & season with salt & pepper.
3. Bake for 45 to 60 minutes at 425 F.

Nutritional information

Carbs: 22 g, Cal: 263 kcal, Prt: 31 g, Fats: 7 g

5.53 Hummus Chicken Salad

Time for cook: 0 minutes, **Complexity level:** easy, **Time for prep.:** 10 minutes, **Portions:** 4

Ingredients

- 2 tbsp. of sliced green onions
- 1 tsp. of lemon juice
- Half a cup of hummus
- 1 tbsp. of chopped parsley
- 2 cooked & chopped chicken breasts
- 1/4 cup of chopped red bell pepper

Directions

1. Add all ingredients to a bowl & mix.
2. Serve with salad greens.

Nutritional information

Carbs: 10 g, Cal: 196 kcal, Prt: 21 g, Fats: 9 g

5.54 Lemon Rosemary Chicken

Time for cook: 26 minutes, **Complexity level:** easy, **Time for prep.:** 10 minutes, **Portions:** 4

Ingredients

- 1 tbsp. of dried rosemary
- 1 lemon, cut into slices
- 1 lemon's zest & juice
- 1 tbsp. of dijon mustard
- 2 cloves of garlic, minced
- 1 lb. of chicken thighs, boneless & skinless

Directions

1. Let the oven preheat to 425 F.
2. Mix garlic, zest, mustard, juice, salt & pepper in a bowl.
3. Add the chicken with lemon slices & rosemary, and coat well.
4. Roast on a baking sheet for 20 to 25 minutes, and serve.

Nutritional information

Carbs: 2 g, Cal: 181 kcal, Prt: 31 g, Fats: 8g

5.55 Egg White Veggie Scramble

Time for cook: 10 minutes, **Complexity level:** easy, **Time for prep.:** 10 minutes, **Portions:** 2

Ingredients

- 2 tbsp. of chopped yellow & red peppers
- 3 egg whites
- Half tbsp. of chopped red onion
- 1 Tbsp. of salsa
- Half a cup of chopped spinach

Directions

1. In a pan, sauté peppers & onion in a splash of oil for 2 to 3 minutes.
2. Add spinach & cook until it wilts.
3. Add egg white & cook to your desired consistency.
4. Serve with salsa.

Nutritional information

Carbs: 7 g, Cal: 110 kcal, Prt: 14 g, Fats: 0 g

5.56 Vegetarian Chili

Time for cook: 30 minutes, **Complexity level:** easy, **Time for prep.:** 20 minutes, **Portions:** 10

Ingredients

- 1 yellow onion, chopped
- 10 oz. of each dark & light red kidney bean, rinsed
- 1 green bell pepper, chopped
- 20 oz. of diced tomatoes
- 1 red bell pepper, chopped
- 2 garlic cloves, minced
- 1 jalapeno pepper, diced without seeds
- 1 butternut squash, chopped
- 1 tbsp. of olive oil
- 1 lb. of medium-firm tofu
- 3 cups of water
- Half tbsp. of chipotle powder
- 10 oz. of black beans, rinsed
- 2 tbsp. of chili powder
- 2 tsp. of lime juice
- Salt & pepper, to taste

Directions

1. Sauté squash, onions, garlic & pepper in hot oil for 10 minutes on medium flame.
2. Add tofu, spices, water, jalapeno peppers, tomatoes & beans. Mix & cook on low for 20 minutes.
3. Add more water if you like more liquid.
4. Serve warm.

Nutritional information

Carbs: 45 g, Cal: 270 kcal, Prt: 31 g, Fats: 2 g

5.57 Spicy Summer Beans & Sausage

Time for cook: 8 hours, **Complexity level:** easy, **Time for prep.:** 20 minutes, **Portions:** 6

Ingredients

- 1 yellow onion, diced
- 2 tomatoes, diced without seeds
- Half tsp. of kosher salt
- 1 tsp. of smoked paprika
- 3 cloves garlic, minced
- 8 oz. of Andouille sausage, chopped
- 1 lb. of Great Northern beans dry
- 4 cups of broth
- 2 tsp. of Cajun spice
- 1 jalapeno pepper, diced
- 2 cups of water

Directions

1. Cook sausage in a splash of oil until browned.
2. Add tomato & onion, and cook for 2 minutes.
3. Add garlic & cook for 1 minute.
4. Add the rest of the ingredients, and mix well. Transfer to crockpot.
5. Cook on low for 8 hours. Serve.

Nutritional information

Carbs: 31 g, Cal: 290 kcal, Prt: 13 g, Fats: 10 g

5.58 Meatless Mexican Frittata

Time for cook: 35 minutes, **Complexity level:** easy, **Time for prep.:** 20 minutes, **Portions:** 6-8

Ingredients

- 1 yellow pepper, chopped
- 1 tsp. of Mexican Spice
- 1 tomato, diced
- 1 green pepper, chopped
- 1 cup of cooked black beans
- Half tsp. of baking powder
- 6 eggs
- 1 yellow onion, cubed
- 1 cup of Shredded Mexican cheese

Directions

1. Let the oven preheat to 350 F.
2. Sauté the tomatoes, peppers & onions in hot oil for 1 to 2 minutes.
3. Add spices & beans.
4. Whisk the eggs with baking powder. Add to the pan, and cook without touching.
5. Spread it on the entire pan. Cook for 8-10 minutes on low flame.
6. Flip & cook for a few more minutes, slice & serve.

Nutritional information

Carbs: 12 g, Cal: 79 kcal, Prt: 13 g, Fats: 7 g

5.59 Greek Turkey Burgers

Time for cook: 12 minutes, **Complexity level:** easy, **Time for prep.:** 20 minutes, **Portions:** 4

Ingredients

- 1/4 cup of sliced mushrooms
- 1/4 cup of sliced red bell pepper
- 1 pound of lean ground turkey
- 1/4 cup of fresh basil leaves
- 2 cloves of garlic
- 1/4 tsp. of each salt & black pepper
- 1/4 cup of sliced onion

Directions

1. Preheat the grill.
2. In a food processor, add all vegetables and pulse until chopped.
3. Add to the turkey with spices, mix & make into patties.
4. Grill the patties for 5 to 6 minutes on one side.
5. Serve.

Nutritional information

Carbs: 12 g, Cal: 199 kcal, Prt: 41 g, Fats: 1 g

5.60 Creamy Gelatin Squares

Time for cook: 10 minutes, **Complexity level:** easy, **Time for prep.:** 3 hours & 20 minutes, **Portions:** 8

Ingredients

- 0.6 oz. of Gelatin (sugar-free)
- 1 1/2 cups of light whipped topping, thawed
- Ice cubes, as needed
- 1 1/2 cups of boiling water
- 1 cup of cold water

Directions

1. Mix the gelatin & boiling water in a bowl until mixed.
2. Add ice cubes to cold water to reach 1 ½ cups.
3. Add to the gelatin mixture, and mix until the ice melts.
4. Transfer to a dish, set in the fridge & add whipped toppings on top.
5. Slice & serve.

Nutritional information

Carbs: 3 g, Cal: 30 kcal, Prt: 2 g, Fats: 2 g

5.61 Zucchini & Onion Quiche

Time for cook: 40 minutes, **Complexity level:** easy, **Time for prep.:** 20 minutes, **Portions:** 8

Ingredients

- 1 cup of long-grain rice, cooked
- 1 zucchini, grated
- 1 cup of shredded Swiss cheese
- 1 onion, chopped
- 1 cup of skim milk
- 1 carrot, grated
- 1 cup of chicken broth
- 3 egg whites
- 1 tsp. of crumbled basil

Directions

1. Let the oven preheat to 425 F.
2. In a bowl, add rice, one egg & 2 tbsp. of cheese. Mix with clean hands & press in a pan.
3. Bake for 5 minutes.
4. In a pan, add broth, basil & vegetables. Cook over medium heat until vegetables are tender and crisp. Turn the heat off.
5. Add egg whites & the rest of the ingredients. Mix & pour on the crust.
6. Bake for 20 to 25 minutes at 350 F.
7. Slice & serve.

Nutritional information

Carbs: 10 g, Cal: 190 kcal, Prt: 7 g, Fats: 1 g

5.62 Miso Avocado and Egg

Time for cook: 10 minutes, **Complexity level:** easy, **Time for prep.:** 10 minutes, **Portions:** 1

Ingredients

- 1 tsp. of miso
- 1 egg
- Half avocado

Directions

1. In a bowl, add miso & avocado. Mash well.
2. In a pot of simmering water, crack the egg & cook for 2 to 3 minutes.
3. Serve with avocado mash.

Nutritional information

Carbs: 8 g, Cal: 202 kcal, Prt: 8 g, Fats: 16 g

5.63 Savory Quinoa Muffins

Time for cook: 10 minutes, **Complexity level:** easy, **Time for prep.:** 10 minutes, **Portions:** 1

Ingredients

- 2 eggs
- 1 1/2 tsp. of baking powder
- 1/4 cup of skim milk
- 2 cups of all-purpose flour
- 1 tsp. of salt
- 4 cups of cooked quinoa, cooled
- Half tsp. of black pepper
- 1/4 cup of canola oil
- Half a cup of crumbled feta
- Half a cup of peas
- 1 cup of chopped fresh spinach
- 1 tsp. of fresh dill
- 1 zucchini, grated

Directions

1. Let the oven preheat to 350 F.
2. Oil spray a muffin pan.
3. Whisk milk, oil & eggs in a bowl.
4. Add the baking powder, flour, pepper & salt to a bowl & mix. Add quinoa.
5. Add the wet-to-dry ingredients, and mix until just combined.
6. Add the rest of the ingredients & mix until just combined.
7. Pour into the pan & bake for half an hour.
8. Serve warm.

Nutritional information

Carbs: 13 g, Cal: 98 kcal, Prt: 3 g, Fats: 3 g

Chapter 6: General Reintroduction of Solid foods

6.1 Angelic Eggs

Time for cook: 10 mins.   **Complexity level:** Easy   **Time for prep.:** 8 mins.   **Portions:** 2

Ingredients

- 1 cup chicken breast
- 2 egg white, hard-boiled
- 3 tbsp unflavored yogurt

- A pinch each of ground black pepper, onion powder, salt, and garlic powder
- 2 tbsp mayo
- Several cherry tomatoes, quartered

Execution

1. Air-fry the chicken at 400°F for almost 10 mins.
2. Using a fork, shred the chicken into smaller bits and set it in a bowl.
3. In a second container, mix in mayonnaise, yogurt, and spices. As required, modify the flavor. Then incorporate it into the chicken mixture.
4. Next, include the tomatoes.
5. Your boiled egg's yolk should be removed and cut in half.
6. Add the chicken salad to the hole within the egg half if you choose.

Nutrition

- Carbs: 7.2 g
- Cal: 239 kcal
- Prt:28.5 g
- Fats: 10.6 g

6.2 Spinach and Mushroom Omelette

Difficulty level: Easy **Preparation time:** 10 minutes **Cooking time:** 10 minutes **Portions:** 2

Ingredients:

- 4 large eggs
- 1 cup fresh spinach, chopped
- 1/2 cup mushrooms, sliced
- 1/4 cup diced onions

- 1/4 cup shredded low-fat cheese (optional)
- Salt and pepper to taste
- Cooking spray or a small amount of olive oil for greasing the pan

Execution:

1. Whisk the eggs in a mixing bowl until well combined and season with salt and pepper to taste.
2. Cooking spray or a small amount of olive oil should be used to lightly grease a nonstick skillet or frying pan over medium heat.
3. Sauté the diced onions and sliced mushrooms in the pan for 3-4 minutes or until they begin to soften.
4. Cook for a few minutes, until the spinach is wilted, in the pan.
5. Pour the beaten eggs into the pan, covering the vegetables evenly.
6. Cook for 2-3 minutes or until the edges of the omelet start to set.
7. If using, sprinkle the shredded low-fat cheese over one side of the omelet.
8. Gently fold the omelet in half, covering the cheese if added, and cook for another 2-3 minutes until the eggs are fully cooked, and the cheese is melted (if using).
9. Slide the omelet onto a plate and cut it in half to serve two portions.
10. Serve hot, and enjoy a delicious and nutritious breakfast!

Nutritional Value per Serving:

- Cal: 160
- Carbs: 5g
- Prt:13g
- Fat: 10g

Note: You can modify this recipe by adding other vegetables or herbs per your preferences and dietary restrictions.

6.3 Apple Fritters

Time for cook: 14 mins.   **Complexity level:** Easy   **Time for prep.:** 9 mins.   **Portions:** 2

Ingredients

For the fritters:

- 1 cup self-rising flour
- 1 tbsp cinnamon
- 2 tsp sugar (optional)

- 1 large, peeled apple
- 1 cup plain yogurt

For the glaze:

- 2 tbsp milk (take more if needed)

- 1 cup confectioners' sugar

Execution

1. Knead the fritter ingredients 3 or 4 times in a bowl to combine.
2. Once more, combine all glaze contents, thin down the mixture, then put it aside.
3. Place oil on the foil-lined bottom of an air fryer basket.
4. Divide the fritter so that it is the size of 4 handballs.
5. Spoon veggie spray over the fritters before placing them within the air fryer basket.
6. Fry in an air fryer for 6-8 mins. at 370°F. Turnover, re-spray, and cook for a further 5–6 mins.
7. Remove them, dip them into the glaze, and then set them to cool on the wire rack.

Nutrition

- Carbs: 73.9 g
- Cal: 348 kcal
- Prt:18 g
- Fats: 9.4 g

6.4 Garlic Cheese Bread

Time for cook: 10 mins.   **Complexity level:** Easy   **Time for prep.:** 5 mins.   **Portions:** 2

Ingredients

- ¼ cup Parmesan cheese
- 1 cup Mozzarella cheese
- 1 egg
- ½ tsp garlic powder

Execution

1. Line the basket for the air fryer with a layer of parchment paper.
2. Mix the Mozzarella, Parmesan, egg, as well as garlic powder in a bowl. Make a circle out of the parchment paper and push it into the air fryer's basket.
3. Bring the air fryer up to temperature, preferably 350°F. Air-fry the bread for 10 mins.

Nutrition

- Carbs: 1.2 g
- Cal: 85 kcal
- Prt:22.2 g
- Fats: 7.8 g

6.5 Flour Tortilla Bowls

Time for cook: 5 mins.   **Complexity level:** Easy   **Time for prep.:** 5 mins.   **Portions:** 1

Ingredients

- 1 (1/8 inch) flour tortilla

- 1 soufflé dish

Execution

1. Heat the tortilla in a broad pan or straight on the burner to get it soft and flexible. Place the tortilla inside a soufflé pan.
2. Air-fry the tortilla for approximately 4–5 mins. at 375°F until it starts turning golden brown.
3. Remove the tortilla bowl from the soufflé dish, then set it upside-down in the basket. Once golden brown, add one to 2 more mins. there in the air fryer.

Nutrition

- Carbs: 10.7 g
- Cal: 52 kcal
- Prt:1.4 g
- Fats: 0.7 g

6.6 Ham and Cheese Turnovers

Time for cook: 10 mins.   **Complexity level:** Easy   **Time for prep.:** 22 mins.   **Portions:** 4

Ingredients

- 1 (13.8 oz) refrigerated pizza crust
- ¼ cup chopped walnuts, toasted
- 1 pear
- 2 tbsp crumbled Blue cheese
- ¼ lb. Deli ham

Execution

1. Set the air fryer to 400°F.
2. Place the pizza crust on a lightly dusted board and unroll it into a 12-inch square. Create 4 squares out of each component. Place a diagonal layer of ham, walnuts, and Blue cheese within ½ inch of each square's borders. Fold one corner out over the filling, then push the edges of the triangle using a fork.
3. In batches, arrange the turnovers just on a greased tray of an air-fryer basket together in one layer and coat with cooking spray. Cook over 4-6 mins. so it appears golden brown on each side. Garnish with additional slices of pear before serving.

Nutrition

- Carbs: 53.9 g
- Cal: 370 kcal
- Prt:15.1 g
- Fats: 11.3 g

6.7 Toast Sticks

Time for cook: 10 mins.   **Complexity level:** Easy   **Time for prep.:** 12 mins.   **Portions:** 2

Ingredients

- 6 Texas toast slices
- 2 tsp cinnamon
- 3 eggs
- 1 tbsp vanilla extract
- ¾ cup heavy cream
- 1/3 cup sugar
- 2 tbsp melted butter

Execution

1. Cut the bread into 3 sticks-like pieces.
2. Combine the egg, vanilla essence, and heavy cream.
3. Blend in the sugar and cinnamon.
4. Be sure to spray the fryer basket with nonstick spray before using it.
5. After dipping the toast sticks there in the egg mixture, place them inside the fryer basket.
6. Follow the cooking time and temperature instructions: 6 mins. at 360°F. The second side should be cooked for an extra 1-3 mins.
7. Take them out and roll them there in the cinnamon-sugar mix before dipping them in melted butter.

Nutrition

- Carbs: 97.9 g
- Cal: 802 kcal
- Prt:14.6 g
- Fats: 37.1 g

6.8 Bacon-Wrapped Jalapeño Poppers

Time for cook: 10 mins.   **Complexity level:** Easy   **Time for prep.:** 5 mins.   **Portions:** 1

Ingredients

- 1 large jalapeño
- 2 bacon strips
- 1 oz cream cheese
- A pinch each of salt and pepper
- 10 g shredded cheddar Cheese

Execution

1. Split jalapeños lengthwise and preheat the air fryer to 325°F. Remove the seeds using a scraper.
2. Mix cream, cheddar cheese, salt, and pepper in a medium bowl. Fill the cheese mixture into your piping bag.
3. Fill the inside of each jalapeño half using the cream cheese mixture.
4. Cover the jalapeño with 1 bacon slice.
5. Cook the jalapeño in the air fryer for 8–10 mins., ensuring the bacon turns crisp.

Nutrition

- Carbs: 2.3 g
- Cal: 349 kcal
- Prt:18.9 g
- Fats: 29.2 g

6.9 Italian Sausages, Pepper, and Onion

Time for cook: 25 mins.   **Complexity level:** Easy   **Time for prep.:** 15 mins.   **Portions:** 4

Ingredients

- 2 onions
- 4 cheese slices
- 1 red bell pepper, sliced
- 4 buns, lightly toasted
- 1 lb Italian sausage
- 1 yellow bell pepper, sliced
- 1 tsp Italian seasoning
- A pinch of ground black pepper
- 1 orange bell pepper, sliced
- A pinch of salt
- 2 tbsp olive oil

Execution

1. First, make sure to preheat your air fryer to 350°F.
2. Next, peel and finely dice your onions, dividing them into halves from roots to stems and, after that, into thirds.
3. Together in a medium-sized bowl, mix the peppers and onions. Add salt, pepper, Italian seasoning, and olive oil.
4. Put the veggies in the air fryer's basket, and place the sausage on top of them without touching them. Time it for 15 mins., and you'll be good to go. After 10 mins., flip the sausages over and continue cooking.
5. Place provolone cheese and vegetables on top of each sausage on a bun.

Nutrition

- Carbs: 32 g
- Cal: 709 kcal
- Prt:34.6 g
- Fats: 49.1 g

6.10 Cilantro Lime Chicken Wings

Time for cook: 15 mins.   **Complexity level:** Easy   **Time for prep.:** 5 mins.   **Portions:** 2

Ingredients

- 4 chicken wings (84 g)
- ½ tsp pepper
- ½ cup fresh cilantro
- 1 red chili
- ½ tsp salt
- 1 tbsp lime juice
- 1 tbsp olive oil
- 1 tbsp lime zest
- 1 garlic clove

Execution

1. Use a food processor to make a smooth paste from cilantro, pepper, chili, salt, garlic, lime juice, zest, and olive oil.
2. Add chicken wings to a bowl, then pour the sauce over them.
3. When finished, cover and chill for a minimum of 30 mins.
4. Spread the chicken wings out in a layer in the air fryer's cooking basket. Cook the wings for 40–15 mins. at 390°F or until they become crisp, golden brown, as well as well cooked.
5. Add lime wedges for serving.

Nutrition

- Carbs: 4.1 g
- Cal: 151 kcal
- Prt:12.1 g
- Fats: 9.9 g

6.11 Salt and Vinegar Fries

Time for cook: 30 mins. **Complexity level:** Easy **Time for prep.:** 10 mins. **Portions:** 1

Ingredients
- 1 potato
- A pinch of black pepper
- ½ tbsp olive oil
- 1 cup distilled white vinegar
- Salt to taste
- ½ cup water

Execution
1. Peel and slice the potato lengthwise into ½-inch pieces. Put potato sticks in the cold, running water for a few seconds. Make room in a big bowl for mixing. Put the potato sticks into a bowl of water and vinegar and let them sit for around 30 mins.
2. Set the air fryer's temperature to 320°F. After tossing, put pepper, olive oil, and salt, and transfer to the fryer basket.
3. Cook for 15 mins. Increase the setting to 355°F. Shake the basket once more and cook for 6 mins., checking to ensure the outsides are brown and crispy.

Nutrition
- Carbs: 66.7 g
- Cal: 395 kcal
- Prt:7.5 g
- Fats: 7.1 g

6.12 Apple Chips

Time for cook: 20 mins. **Complexity level:** Easy **Time for prep.:** 10 mins. **Portions:** 2

Ingredients
- ½ tbsp chile-lime seasonings
- 1 apple, cored

Execution
1. Slice the apple very thinly with a mandolin.
2. Arrange as many apple slices as possible in the air fryer basket, ensuring they don't touch each other.
3. Cook at 180°F for 40 mins. After flipping the apple slices, remove the basket and simmer for a further 8–40 mins. Apply chile-lime seasoning immediately.

Nutrition
- Carbs: 15.4 g
- Cal: 58 kcal
- Prt:4.4 g
- Fats: 0.3 g

6.13 Latkes

Time for cook: 10 mins. **Complexity level:** Easy **Time for prep.:** 10 mins. **Portions:** 4

Ingredients
- 1 lb potatoes, peeled and grated
- Pepper to taste
- 2 eggs
- Nonstick cooking spray
- ½ onion, sliced
- Salt to taste
- ¼ cup seasoned breadcrumbs

Execution
1. Refine any surplus liquid from the potatoes using a fresh kitchen towel. Combine potatoes, salt, eggs, onion, breadcrumbs, and pepper.
2. Spray some cooking spray on the air fryer basket. Place 1/4 cup of the potato mix in the basket. Spray the tops with a nonstick spray.
3. Air fry for 8–40 mins. at 375°F. Fry them up until they're crunchy and browned.

Nutrition
- Carbs: 24.4 g
- Cal: 149 kcal
- Prt:6.3 g
- Fats: 3.2 g

6.14 Okra Fries

Time for cook: 15 mins. **Complexity level:** Easy **Time for prep.:** 10 mins. **Portions:** 2

Ingredients
- 1 lb fresh okra
- Seasoned salt to taste
- 1 ½ tsp olive oil

Execution
1. Clean, dry, and halve the okra lengthwise after removing the stems and ends. Pour some olive oil and some seasoned salt and toss the ingredients together.
2. Once the fryer has hit 400°F, cook the okra slices through an air fryer's basket with the cut side down for 10–40 mins.

Nutrition
- Carbs: 16.9 g
- Cal: 181 kcal
- Prt:4.4 g
- Fats: 10.9 g

6.15 Chicken Quesadilla Pizza

Time for cook: 10 mins.   **Complexity level:** Easy   **Time for prep.:** 6 mins.   **Portions:** 1

Ingredients

- 2 tbsp pizza sauce
- 4 tbsp caviar
- ¼ cup shredded taco blend cheese
- 1 oz roasted chicken
- 1 multigrain flatbread

Execution

1. Lay the flatbread out on the baking sheet and let it air dry for several mins. to make it crispier. Remove the crust, then spread the pizza sauce on top.
2. Arrange the bite-sized chunks of meat over the crust before adding the caviar.
3. Cover the pie's top with an even layer of cheese. Just pop it back again into the air fryer for another 5 mins. if you want to eat it straight away.

Nutrition

- Carbs: 15.3 g
- Cal: 340 kcal
- Prt:33.4 g
- Fats: 16.9 g

6.16 Onion Rings

Time for cook: 10 mins.   **Complexity level:** Easy   **Time for prep.:** 6 mins.   **Portions:** 2

Ingredients

- 1/2 cup all-purpose flour
- Cooking spray
- 1/4 cup buttermilk
- ½ cup Panko breadcrumbs
- ¼ tsp sea salt
- ½ sweet onion, cut into rings
- 1/2 egg

Execution

1. In a bowl, mix the salt and flour. In a separate bowl, whisk the buttermilk and egg together. Place the breadcrumbs in a third shallow bowl.
2. Flour onion rings and lightly coat, drain any excess liquid after submerging onion rings inside the buttermilk mixture, and spread out the Panko breadcrumbs evenly over the onion.
3. After coating them with cooking spray, arrange them together in a single layer within the air fryer basket.
4. In an air fryer that has been prepared, cook for approx nine to 10 mins. at about 375°F.

Nutrition

- Carbs: 48.3 g
- Cal: 266 kcal
- Prt:9.6 g
- Fats: 3.4 g

6.17 Avocado Oil Tater Tots

Time for cook: 15 mins.   **Complexity level:** Easy   **Time for prep.:** 6 mins.   **Portions:** 2

Ingredients

- 8 oz frozen tater tots
- 1 tbsp avocado oil
- Salt to taste

Execution

1. Drizzle some avocado oil over the frozen tots. Add a dash of salt and blend by tossing.
2. Cook for 15 mins. at 400°F inside an air fryer that has been preheated, rotating the food in the basket after 5 mins. If you prefer them crispier, extend the cooking time.

Nutrition

- Carbs: 27 g
- Cal: 278 kcal
- Prt:2.7 g
- Fats: 17

6.18 Chocolate and Salted Cocoa Peanut Butter Cup

Time for cook: 25 mins.   **Complexity level:** Easy   **Time for prep.:** 5 mins.   **Portions:** 1

Ingredients

- 8 oz milk
- 2 tsp butterscotch pudding
- 1 tbsp chocolate flavor syrup
- A pinch of kosher salt
- 1 pack of cocoa mix
- 1 scoop Protein powder
- 2–3 tbsp peanut butter syrup

Execution

1. Set the air fryer to 300°F.
2. Pour the necessary amount of milk into a blender. Next, introduce the remaining items you have.
3. Mix thoroughly. Fill a cup with the mixture.
4. Mix it. Warm in the fryer for about 1–2 mins. To finish it off, add a dollop of whipped cream.

Nutrition

- Carbs: 65.5 g
- Cal: 613 kcal
- Prt:39.8 g
- Fats: 22.8 g

6.19 Corn Pudding

Time for cook: 55 mins.   **Complexity level:** hard   **Time for prep.:** 12 mins.   **Portions:** 1

Ingredients

- 1 egg
- ¼ package of muffin mix
- 1 tsp onion powder
- 1/4 cup Greek yogurt
- ½ cup creamed corn
- 1 tbsp no-calorie sweetener
- 2 bacon slices, cooked
- ¼ cup cheddar cheese
- ½ cup kernel corn
- 1/4 cup baking mix
- 1 tsp garlic powder

Execution

1. For best results, set your air fryer to 325°F.
2. Thoroughly combine Greek yogurt, egg, corn, salt, butter, onion powder, Splenda, and garlic powder.
3. Fold in the cheese, Atkins baking mix, corn muffin mix, crumbled bacon, and protein powder. Together, stir them.
4. Pour mixture into fryer basket; cook for 45 mins.
5. Sprinkle the remaining cheese on top and re-cook for a further 5–10 mins. to melt it.

Nutrition

- Carbs: 71.5 g
- Cal: 561 kcal
- Prt:27 g
- Fats: 19.3 g

6.20 Grilled Pear with Herbs and Cheese

Time for cook: 10 mins.   **Complexity level:** Easy   **Time for prep.:** 5 mins.   **Portions:** 2

Ingredients

- 1 tbsp olive oil
- ¼ cup Ricotta Cheese
- ¼ cup sliced almonds
- 2 tbsp sugar-free caramel sauce
- ½ tbsp fresh basil chopped
- 2 Cheddar cheese wedges
- 1 pear, halved
- 1 tbsp butter

Execution

1. Set the time in the air fryer to 8–10 mins. at about 320°F. Cook pears by coating them with butter.
2. Combine Ricotta and Cheddar cheeses in one bowl. Add the basil and stir. Give your mixture some time to chill.
3. Roast almond slices.
4. Place a slice of pear on one of the platters. Now add cheese, caramel sauce, toasted almonds, and basil.

Nutrition

- Carbs: 34.3 g
- Cal: 507 kcal
- Prt:20.9 g
- Fats: 33.7 g

6.21 Mozzarella Sticks

Time for cook: 10 mins.   **Complexity level:** Easy   **Time for prep.:** 5 mins.   **Portions:** 1

Ingredients

- 1/4 cup high-fiber cereal
- A pinch of black pepper
- 2 tbsp spaghetti sauce or marinara
- A pinch of Italian seasoning (optional)
- 1 tbsp wheat breadcrumbs
- A pinch of onion salt
- 1 1/2 Mozzarella cheese sticks
- 1/2 beaten egg
- 1 tbsp grated Parmesan cheese
- A pinch of onion powder
- ¼ cup water

Execution

1. Set your air fryer to 300°F.
2. Combine crushed cereal, spices, breadcrumbs, and Parmesan cheese in one dish. Mix everything well.
3. Whisk egg and water in one dish.
4. Dip each cheese wedge into the egg, followed by the crumb mixture.
5. Cook until crispy for a little under 10 mins.

Nutrition

- Carbs: 68.8 g
- Cal: 805 kcal
- Prt:35.9 g
- Fats: 48 g

6.22 Cinnamon Churros

Time for cook: 10 mins.   **Complexity level:** Difficult   **Time for prep.:** 10 mins.   **Portions:** 4

Ingredients

- 1 cup water
- 2 tbsp vegetable oil
- ½ cup white sugar to taste
- 1 tsp ground cinnamon
- Cooking spray
- 1 cup all-purpose flour
- ½ tsp salt
- 2 ½ tbsp white sugar

Execution

1. Bring water, sugar, salt, and vegetable oil to a boil in a small pot. When the dough becomes a ball, gradually add the flour.
2. Spray the air fryer. Put 5–6-inch strips of the dough into the basket using a sturdy pastry bagpipe. At 400°F, cook for 5–7 mins.
3. In a dish, mix sugar and cinnamon. Roll churros over this mixture.

Nutrition

- Carbs: 49.3 g
- Cal: 269 kcal
- Prt:3.3 g
- Fats: 7.1 g

6.23 Panko-Crusted Mahi-Mahi

Time for cook: 15 mins.   **Complexity level:** Difficult   **Time for prep.:** 5 mins.   **Portions:** 4

Ingredients

- 4 mahi-mahi fillets
- 1 lemon wedge
- 2 tbsp grapeseed oil
- ½ tsp ground turmeric
- 1 tsp chopped fresh parsley
- 2 cups panko breadcrumbs
- Nonstick cooking spray
- 1 tbsp bagel seasoning
- ½ tsp black pepper
- ½ tsp garlic salt

Execution

1. Place mahi-mahi fillets on a platter and cover them with grapeseed oil.
2. Combine panko, pepper, bagel seasoning, turmeric, and garlic salt on a shallow plate.
3. After coating each fillet with the panko mixture, place it in the air fryer.
4. Coat the pan with nonstick spray, then cook the fish in an air fryer at over 400°F for 40–15 mins., flipping the fish halfway through until it flakes readily with a fork.
5. Garnish the dish with lemon and parsley.

Nutrition

- Carbs: 52.8 g
- Cal: 440 kcal
- Prt:30.9 g
- Fats: 11 g

6.24 Sausage Patties

Time for cook: 10 mins.   **Complexity level:** Easy   **Time for prep.:** 5 mins.   **Portions:** 4

Ingredients

- 1 (12 oz) package of sausage patties
- Nonstick cooking spray

Execution

1. Set the air fryer to 400°F.
2. Arrange the sausage patties in a layer in the frying basket.
3. Cook together in the air fryer for more than 5 mins. Remove the basket, turn the sausage over, and cook for an additional 3 mins.

Nutrition

- Carbs: 0 g
- Cal: 269 kcal
- Prt:13.4 g
- Fats

6.25 Tots

Time for cook: 10 mins.   **Complexity level:** Easy   **Time for prep.:** 5 mins.   **Portions:** 4

Ingredients

- 36 potato nuggets

Direction

1. Preheat the air fryer for 4 mins. at 350°F.
2. Put the necessary amount of potato nuggets inside this fryer basket in a layer.
3. Set the timer for around 6 mins. Gently shake the basket. Cook for an extra 4 mins. until the desired doneness is attained and until the food is crispy.

Nutrition

- Carbs: 171 g
- Cal: 1620 kcal
- Prt:9 g
- Fats: 99 g

6.26 Cheesy Pigs

Time for cook: 7 mins.   **Complexity level:** Easy   **Time for prep.:** 12 mins.   **Portions:** 8

Ingredients

- 1 tube of crescent rolls refrigerated
- 1 tbsp unsalted butter
- 1 cup Mozzarella shredded
- 2 tsp sesame seeds
- 8 hot dogs

Execution

1. After unrolling, divide the dough into 8 triangles.
2. Use enough Mozzarella cheese to thoroughly encase each triangle. At the triangles' wide ends, roll in the hot dogs.
3. Spread melted butter on the rolls, then sprinkle sesame seeds at the top.
4. Select "Bake" and program the timer for 7 mins. at 375°F. Press the "Start" button to get started.
5. Cover the pigs in the basket with a blanket when preheating. Make sure there is enough space between them, so they don't bump against each other.
6. After the cooking period is through, transfer them to a serving tray. Enjoy!

Nutrition

- Carbs: 4.4 g
- Cal: 182 kcal
- Prt:6.4 g
- Fats: 15.4 g

6.27 Dumplings

Time for cook: 10 mins.   **Complexity level:** Easy   **Time for prep.:** 5 mins.   **Portions:** 2

Ingredients
- 8 oz vegetable, pork, or frozen chicken dumplings

For the dipping sauce:
- 1/4 cup water
- 1/8 cup maple syrup
- ½ tsp rice vinegar
- 1/4 cup soy sauce
- A small pinch of red pepper flakes
- 1/2 tsp garlic powder

Execution
1. Set a timer on for 4 mins. and prep food in an air fryer at about 370°F.
2. Oil the inside of the fryer, then put the frozen dumplings on top of one another.
3. Cook for an additional 5 mins., then shake a basket and add more oil.
4. Cook the dumplings for an extra 4-6 mins. until they finish.
5. Convert the remaining ingredients into a dipping sauce in the interim.
6. Remove the dumplings from the basket; leave them alone for a further 2 mins. before serving.

Nutrition
- Carbs: 24.2 g
- Cal: 148 kcal
- Prt:5.5 g
- Fats: 3.5 g

6.29 Fried Dill Pickle

Time for cook: 10 mins.   **Complexity level:** Easy   **Time for prep.:** 5 mins.   **Portions:** 1

Ingredients

- ¼ cup buttermilk
- 1/4 cup all-purpose flour
- ¼ cup cornmeal
- Cooking spray as needed
- ¼ tsp garlic powder
- 2 oz dill pickle chips

Execution

1. Heat your air fryer to 400°F.
2. Pickles and buttermilk should be combined in one bowl and stirred to coat.
3. Combine flour, cornmeal, and garlic powder in a separate basin.
4. Drain the buttermilk from your pickles. Add the pickles and stir the cornmeal mixture to coat them completely.
5. Place pickles in the air fryer basket together in layers and spray with frying spray.
6. Set a 10-minute timer to cook pickles until the coating turns crispy.

Nutrition

- Carbs: 81.1 g
- Cal: 580 kcal
- Prt:11.9 g
- Fats: 22.8 g

6.30 Lemon Bars

Time for cook: 30 mins.   **Complexity level:** Medium   **Time for prep.:** 15 mins.   **Portions:** 1

Ingredients

- Juice of 2/3 lemon
- 1/16 cup Splenda
- 1/4 egg yolks
- 0.08 tbsp cornstarch
- 0.08 cup egg substitute

For the crust:

- 0.08 cup high-fiber cereal
- 0.08 cup coconut flour
- A pinch of salt
- 0.42 oz cream cheese
- 0.17 tbsp Splenda

Execution

1. Heat your air fryer to 325°F.
2. Spray your nonstick cooking oil all over the air fryer.
3. Combine coconut flour, sweetener, salt, and cereal in one bowl to create the filling. Include softened cream cheese until the mixture resembles a clumpy mixture that could be shaped into loose balls.
4. Set a 15-minute timer to cook the crust, then cool it.
5. Combine egg yolks, sweetener, liquid egg substitute, and lemon. Completely combine everything in the blender. Add the cornstarch at this point, stirring again.
6. Pour this lemon mixture over the crust and bake for 25-30 mins. so that the lemon custard thickens.
7. After the bars have cooled, cut them into squares and store them there in the fridge.

Nutrition

- Carbs: 19.6 g
- Cal: 155 kcal
- Prt:3.1 g
- Fats: 5.9 g

6.31 Mexican Peppers and Sausage

Time for cook: 25 mins.   **Complexity level:** Easy   **Time for prep.:** 5 mins.   **Portions:** 1

Ingredients

- 1 spicy jalapeño chicken sausage
- ½ small onion
- ¼ cup Mexican cheese blend
- 1/3 cup salsa
- ¼ green pepper

Execution

1. Heat your air fryer to 380°F.
2. Set a 15-minute timer to cook the sausage while also sautéing the onions and peppers.
3. After moving the sausage to the cutting board, slice it into pieces.
4. Combine the sausage chunks with the onions as well as peppers.
5. Once everything has been thoroughly combined, whisk in your salsa.
6. Place on a serving tray and sprinkle with cheese.

Nutrition

- Carbs: 16.2 g
- Cal: 250 kcal
- Prt:14.5 g
- Fats: 14.5 g

6.32 Plantain Chips

Time for cook: 25 mins.   **Complexity level:** Easy   **Time for prep.:** 5 mins.   **Portions:** 1

Ingredients

- 3 plantains
- 2 tsp vegetable oil
- 1 tsp sea salt
- Zest of 1 lime
- ½ tsp garlic powder (optional)
- 1/8 tsp chili powder

Execution

1. Make a couple of slits in each plantain to separate them. Use a mandolin to make thin, diagonal slices of the plantains to increase surface area. Mix the plantains and other ingredients (oil and spices) in a bowl.
2. Heat your air fryer to 374°F. Cook immediately with a timer set for 15-20 mins.; after 5 mins., give it a nice shake, and take out any crispy or burnt chips.

Nutrition

- Carbs: 172.5 g
- Cal: 741 kcal
- Prt:7.3 g
- Fats: 11.1 g

6.33 Protein Pumpkin Custard

Time for cook: 35 mins.   **Complexity level:** Easy   **Time for prep.:** 5 mins.   **Portions:** 1

Ingredients

- 2 egg whites
- ¾ cup of no-calorie sweetener
- 2 whey protein
- 2/3 cup milk
- ½ tsp pumpkin pie spice
- 1 cup pumpkin puree

Execution

1. Heat your air fryer to 325°F.
2. Whisk Egg whites there in a single bowl until foamy.
3. Combine sweetener and the above ingredients by whisking them together. Mix the protein, then go through the process once more.
4. Mix the pumpkin puree and pumpkin pie spice thoroughly.
5. Include just enough evaporated milk so that the mixture is lump-free.
6. Spoon the mixture into ramekins and heat for approx 30 mins., just until foamy.
7. Sprinkle some whipped cream over it.

Nutrition

- Carbs: 18.9 g
- Cal: 221 kcal
- Prt:29.8 g
- Fats: 4 g

6.34 Parmesan Ravioli

Time for cook: 6 mins.   **Complexity level:** Easy   **Time for prep.:** 5 mins.   **Portions:** 2

Ingredients

- 3 oz ravioli
- ¼ cup Italian breadcrumbs
- Marinara sauce
- 1/2 tbsp grated Parmesan cheese
- 1/2 egg beat
- 1/4 cup milk
- ¼ tbsp fresh parsley

Execution

1. Combine the milk and egg separately. Place the breadcrumbs in a separate dish.
2. Place your ravioli inside this egg mixture there, allowing any extra drop off, then add the breadcrumb mixture.
3. Set your air fryer up to 380°F for preheating; cook for about 5-6 mins., turning once halfway through.
4. Right before serving, parmesan cheese was sprinkled on top of the ravioli. Accompany with marinara sauce and fresh parsley.

Nutrition

- Carbs: 50.4 g
- Cal: 727 kcal
- Prt:25.8 g
- Fats: 36.1 g

6.35 Ramekin Shepherd's Pie

Time for cook: 20 mins.   **Complexity level:** Easy   **Time for prep.:** 10 mins.   **Portions:** 1

Ingredients

- 1/8 yellow onion
- 1/8 bag of frozen cauliflower florets
- Salt to taste
- 1/12 cup Cheddar cheese
- 2 oz peas and carrots (canned)
- ½ laughing cow cheese
- 1 oz mushroom soup cream
- Pepper to taste
- 1/8 lb ground meat, lean

Execution

1. Put nonstick oil into our air fryer and warm it to only 325°F. Add the onions and cook for 2 mins.
2. When the ground beef is cooked, brown it and combine it with the onions for around 10 mins. Drain. Cauliflower florets must be added to a saucepan of boiling water.
3. Add your carrots and peas. After that, add the soup and mix it in. Add a ¼ cup of milk if the soup isn't thick enough. Before removing the mixture from the fire, let it fully boil.
4. Combine cauliflower and slices of laughing cow in a mash.
5. Add a quarter of the way up with a meat/vegetable mash, then top with the cauliflower combination and grated cheese. Set a timer for 10-15 mins. and cook until the cheese is melted.

Nutrition

- Carbs: 32 g
- Cal: 328 kcal
- Prt:27.4 g
- Fats: 10 g

6.36 Refrigerator Pickles

Time for cook: 15 mins.   **Complexity level:** Easy   **Time for prep.:** 5 mins.   **Portions:** 1

Ingredients

- 5 lb pickling cucumbers
- 2 tbsp ground kosher salt
- 5 dill or 6 sprigs
- 2 tsp red pepper flakes
- 6 garlic cloves
- 2 tbsp pickling spice
- 4 cups white vinegar
- 2 cups water

Execution

1. Well-rinsed the cucumbers in a colander. Warm your air fryer up to 325°F. Combine and steam water and vinegar. Remove from flame; add salt, pickling spice, garlic, and red pepper flakes; steam just it's done and appears soft. Give it some time to cool.
2. Fill a gallon canning jar halfway with dill and then cucumbers. When the brining liquid has cooled, pour it over the cucumbers and carefully close the container.
3. Let it rest on the counter for a while, then place it in the refrigerator for 3 days before eating.

Nutrition

- Carbs: 104 g
- Cal: 603 kcal
- Prt:17.3 g
- Fats: 3.4 g

6.37 Spicy Bean Dip with Eggplant

Time for cook: 10 mins.   **Complexity level:** Easy   **Time for prep.:** 5 mins.   **Portions:** 2

Ingredients

- 1/2 can of black beans
- 1/2 can of tomatoes
- 1/2 eggplant, sliced
- ½ can of red onion
- 1/2 can of corn
- ½ can of green chiles
- 4 oz Italian dressing
- ½ can of green bell pepper
- ½ can of black-eyed peas

Execution

1. Set your air fryer's settings to 350°F.
2. Use nonstick spray to coat your air fryer, then cook the eggplant slices for 10 mins. until they become crispy.
3. After washing and drying the corn, combine it with the beans in one bowl. Drain your tomatoes, then introduce them to the dish along with the chiles.
4. Chop up the green bell pepper and onion, then combine them with the beans in a mixing bowl. Place the Italian dressing. Stir it, then put it in the fridge for the night.
5. Place a salad on your eggplant bread and indulge.

Nutrition

- Carbs: 59.4 g
- Cal: 309 kcal
- Prt:15.9 g
- Fats: 2.8 g

6.38 Roasted Garlic

Time for cook: 20 mins.   **Complexity level:** Easy   **Time for prep.:** 7 mins.   **Portions:** 4

Ingredients

- 1 garlic head
- ¼ tsp salt
- 1 tsp virgin olive oil
- ¼ tsp ground black pepper
- Aluminum foil

Execution

1. Heat the air fryer to 380°F.
2. Place the garlic head on a piece of aluminum foil once the top has been removed. Wrap the garlic cloves with foil.
3. Air-fry garlic for sixteen to 20 mins. until it becomes soft, drizzle olive oil after the salt and pepper. Fold the corners of the foil out over the garlic to make a pouch. Too hasty of an opening of the foil might cause the hot steam within to escape.

Nutrition

- Carbs: 11.3 g
- Cal: 61 kcal
- Prt:2.2 g
- Fats: 1.3 g

6.39 Pasta Chips

Time for cook: 40 mins.   **Complexity level:** Medium   **Time for prep.:** 5 mins.   **Portions:** 8

Ingredients

- 2 cups farfalle pasta
- ½ tsp salt
- ½ cup grated Parmesan cheese
- 1 tsp garlic powder
- 1 tsp Italian seasoning
- 1 tbsp olive oil

Execution

1. Heat your air fryer to 400°F to cook food. Lightly salt water in a large pot and heat to a boil. Boil the farfalle pasta for 8 mins., occasionally stirring, until and unless it's just tender yet firm. Simply drain the water without rinsing it. Wait 2 mins., then drain the pasta and toss it with olive oil in a large bowl. Add the Italian seasoning, salt, Parmesan cheese, and garlic powder. Stir everything together thoroughly.
2. Cook the pasta in the air fryer basket in 5-minute batches. After turning with a spatula, cook for an extra 2–3 mins. Put them together on a plate. Any pasta chips that have stuck together need to be broken apart. Continually use the remaining pasta. Allow for complete chilling before crisping.

Nutrition

- Carbs: 17.9 g
- Cal: 116 kcal
- Prt:4.2 g
- Fats: 3 g

6.40 Zucchini Chips

Time for cook: 24 mins.   **Complexity level:** Easy   **Time for prep.:** 12 mins.   **Portions:** 4

Ingredients

- 1 cup panko breadcrumbs
- 1 large egg, beaten
- 1 medium zucchini
- Cooking spray
- ¾ cup Parmesan cheese, grated

Execution

1. Set the air fryer to 350°F and combine the panko and Parmesan cheese in a bowl. Coat one zucchini segment with panko after being dipped into a beaten egg and then the panko mixture.
2. Coat zucchini slices well with cooking spray, then repeat for the remaining pieces. Place as many zucchini segments as you can in the fryer basket without touching one another.
3. Cook for 10 mins. Flip them with tongs. Cook for an additional 2 mins. Take out zucchini slices from the fryer, and use the remaining bits.

Nutrition

- Carbs: 21.3 g
- Cal: 147 kcal
- Prt:7.3 g
- Fats: 3.7 g

6.41 Cinnamon Almonds

Time for cook: 25 mins.   **Complexity level:** Easy   **Time for prep.:** 17 mins.   **Portions:** 2

Ingredients

- 1 egg white
- ½ tsp ground cinnamon
- 2 cups unblanched almonds
- 3 tbsp packed brown sugar
- 1 tbsp vanilla extract
- ½ tsp salt
- 3 tbsp sugar

Execution

1. Set your air fryer to 300°F.
2. Whip the egg whites in a bowl until frothy before stirring in the vanilla extract. Add almonds and stir a little to coat them. Combine the cinnamon, sugars, and salt; gently toss through into the nut mix to coat.
3. Place almonds in one layer in a fryer basket over an oiled baking sheet. Almonds should be crispy after 25–30 mins. of cooking and once-through stirring. Cool. Maintain the container's seal.

Nutrition

- Carbs: 53 g
- Cal: 697 kcal
- Prt:21.9 g
- Fats: 47.5 g

6.42 Oreos

Time for cook: 5 mins.   **Complexity level:** Easy   **Time for prep.:** 5 mins.   **Portions:** 9

Ingredients

- ½ cup pancake mix
- 1/3 cup water
- Cooking spray
- 9 chocolate sandwich cookies
- 1 tbsp confectioners' sugar

Execution

1. Prepare the air fryer for cooking; line the inner basket with baking paper and grease it with cooking spray.
2. Meanwhile, in a dish, combine the water and the pancake mix in the amount indicated in your list.
3. Dip the cookies into the newly created mixture, and you are ready for the baking step (8 mins. at 400°F). Remember to flip the cookies after about 4 mins.
4. Proceed in this manner until the cookies are finished; garnish with powdered sugar before serving.

Nutrition

- Carbs: 30.4 g
- Cal: 188 kcal
- Prt:6.4 g
- Fats: 2.5 g

6.43 Funnel Cake

Time for cook: 10 mins.   **Complexity level:** Medium   **Time for prep.:** 22 mins.   **Portions:** 4

Ingredients

- Nonstick cooking spray
- 1 cup + 1 tbsp almond flour, divided
- 4 tbsp Erythritol confectioners' sweetener
- 1 cup plain Greek yogurt
- 1 tsp ground cinnamon
- 1 ½ tsp baking powder
- ½ tsp salt
- 1 tsp vanilla extract

Execution

1. Combine the Greek yogurt, baking powder, cinnamon, salt, and vanilla extract with the almond flour and 2 tbsp sugar. It would be best if you used your hands to beat the dough.
2. Flour your work area, divide the dough into 4 same-sized portions, and roll each into a ball. Divide each ball into 8 equally sized pieces. After coating each piece in flour, roll it between your palms into a long, thin rope. One by one, arrange all 8 long ropes in a circular pile in the basket of the air fryer that has been constructed. Continue by using the remaining dough balls. Each funnel cake should be coated with frying spray.
3. Air-fried at 325°F for 5–6 mins. or until golden brown. After flipping each funnel cake, spray it with cooking spray and continue air-frying it for 3–4 mins. On top, sprinkle the final 2 tsp of sweetener.

Nutrition

- Carbs: 17.5 g
- Cal: 327 kcal
- Prt:8.2 g
- Fats: 17.5 g

6.44 Muffin Pizzas

Time for cook: 5 mins.   **Complexity level:** Easy   **Time for prep.:** 7 mins.   **Portions:** 8

Ingredients

- 4 English muffins
- Pizza sauce of choice
- Toppings of choice
- ½ cup Mozzarella cheese

Execution

1. Set your air fryer to 400°F.
2. After the fryer has warmed up, place half the muffins inside for about 1 minute.
3. Remove and then add the cheese, sauce, and toppings.
4. Place in the air fryer again and cook for an additional 4–5 mins.

Nutrition

- Carbs: 13.1 g
- Cal: 95 kcal
- Prt:4.3 g
- Fats: 2.9 g

6.45 Chocolate Cake

Time for cook: 15 mins.   **Complexity level:** Easy   **Time for prep.:** 12 mins.   **Portions:** 4

Ingredients

- Cooking spray
- 3 ½ tbsp softened butter
- ¼ cup white sugar
- 1 tbsp apricot jam
- 1 egg
- 1 tbsp unsweetened cocoa powder
- 6 tbsp all-purpose flour
- Salt to taste

Execution

1. Create a whipped mixture by combining sugar and butter and adding egg and jam in several steps.
2. Meanwhile, combine cocoa, salt, and flour in an appropriately sized bowl. Combine the two prepared compounds until you create one well-blended mix.
3. Pour the created mix into an air fryer pan and proceed to the baking step (fifteen mins. at 320°F).

Nutrition

- Carbs: 25.5 g
- Cal: 210 kcal
- Prt:3 g
- Fats: 11.5 g

6.46 Stuffed Apples

Time for cook: 20 mins.   **Complexity level:** Easy   **Time for prep.:** 12 mins.   **Portions:** 1

Ingredients

- 1 apple
- 2 tbsp chopped walnuts
- 2 tbsp raisins
- 1 tsp white sugar
- ½ tbsp unsalted butter
- ½ tsp ground cinnamon
- ½ tsp vanilla extract
- ¼ cup water
- A pinch of ground nutmeg

Execution

1. Cut a 1/2-inch circle around the top of the apple. Take out some of the interiors using a spoon.
2. Combine the raisins, sugar, butter, walnuts, cinnamon, vanilla, and nutmeg.
3. Place a scoop inside the apple. Place the apple in a small oven-safe dish halfway filled with water.
4. Put the dish in the air fryer basket that has been heated up, and cook it for 20–25 mins. at 350°F.

Nutrition

- Carbs: 53 g
- Cal: 353 kcal
- Prt:5.2 g
- Fats: 16.3 g

6.47 Chewy Pecan Cookies

Time for cook: 20 mins.   **Complexity level:** Easy   **Time for prep.:** 5 mins.   **Portions:** 1

Ingredients

- 1 tsp pecan butter
- 1 tsp no-calorie sweetener
- 1 tbsp almond flour
- A pinch salt
- A pinch of vanilla extract
- 1 tbsp milk
- 1 pecan halves

Execution

1. Mix all the ingredients (apart from the pecan halves) in a mixing bowl and blend well.
2. Put a pecan in the dough's middle.
3. Cook for about 20 mins. at 325°F in the air fryer.

Nutrition

- Carbs: 13.7 g
- Cal: 242 kcal
- Prt:5.3 g
- Fats: 18 g

6.48 Low-Sugar Peppermint Mocca Cookies

Time for cook: 15 mins. | **Complexity level:** Easy | **Time for prep.:** 12 mins. | **Portions:** 2

Ingredients

- ½ cup almond flour
- ¼ tsp baking powder
- ¼ tsp salt
- ¼ avocado
- ¼ tsp baking cocoa
- ½ tbsp granular sweetener
- ¼ tsp instant coffee
- 1/2 egg
- ¼ tsp vanilla extract

Execution

1. Mix almond flour, salt, cocoa, baking powder, and instant coffee.
2. Combine the avocado and sugar in a separate bowl to eliminate any avocado lumps, preferably with a hand mixer. Add the vanilla and egg after everything has been thoroughly mixed.
3. Completely blend the dry and wet ingredients, ensuring no lumps. It needs to be chilled for 30 mins.
4. Bake the discs for 12 mins. at 325°F in a preheated air fryer.

Nutrition

- Carbs: 17.5 g
- Cal: 265 kcal
- Prt:10 g
- Fats: 20.8 g

6.49 Low-Sugar Cookie Base

Time for cook: 12 mins. | **Complexity level:** Easy | **Time for prep.:** 5 mins. | **Portions:** 1

Ingredients

- 1 tbsp almond flour
- A pinch of salt
- A pinch of baking powder
- 1 drop of pure vanilla extract
- 1 tsp granular sweetener
- 2 tbsp beaten egg
- 1 tsp unsalted butter, softened

Execution

1. Take two bowls. In the first, combine baking powder, salt, and almond flour;
2. In the second bowl, mix butter and sugar, and when well blended, add egg and vanilla and continue mixing. Combine the two created mixtures to form one and place them in the refrigerator for half an hour.
3. When the time indicated above has elapsed, prepare a baking pan and, helping yourself with a spoon, create disks of the mixture.
4. Moving on to the baking stage, fry the prepared disks in an air fryer (12 mins. at 325°F). When all the cookies are cooked, let them cool for a few mins. and serve.

Nutrition

- Carbs: 3 g
- Cal: 76 kcal
- Prt:3.9 g
- Fats: 5.5 g

6.50 Peanut Butter Cookies

Time for cook: 15 mins. | **Complexity level:** Easy | **Time for prep.:** 5 mins. | **Portions:** 1

Ingredients

- 1 tbsp creamy peanut butter
- ¼ tsp pure vanilla extract
- ¼ egg white
- 1 tbsp brown sugar
- A pinch of cinnamon
- 2 tbsp almond flour

Execution

1. Combine the egg white, brown sugar, cinnamon, vanilla extract, and peanut butter in the mixing bowl. Mix everything thoroughly.
2. Add the almond flour and blend well by folding.
3. Create balls, then space them on the baking sheet by about 2 inches. Flatten the ball into a disc with a fork to create a crisscross design on the cookie's surface.
4. Bake for about 15 mins. in a 325°F preheated air fryer.

Nutrition

- Carbs: 15 g
- Cal: 208 kcal
- Prt:7 g
- Fats: 13.4 g

6.51 Thumb Print Cookies

Time for cook: 25 mins. | **Complexity level:** Easy | **Time for prep.:** 7 mins. | **Portions:** 1

Ingredients

- 2 tbsp cream cheese
- 1/4 egg white
- 1 tbsp brown sugar
- 1 tsp chopped walnuts
- 1 tbsp almond flour
- 1 tsp sugar-free jelly
- 1/2 tsp vanilla extract
- A pinch of salt

Execution

1. In a bowl, put the cream cheese, sugar, egg white, and egg and start mixing.
2. In a second bowl, put the dry items from your ingredient list, salt, almond flour, and vanilla.
3. When the two mixtures are well blended, combine them together to form one.
4. Meanwhile, in a dish, separate one egg by removing the yolk.
5. After fifteen mins., when you have finished blending the mixture, create balls and dip them in the egg white and coat them with walnuts.
6. When you are ready to bake your cookies, arrange them in the air fryer, and all you have to do is bake them (fifteen mins. at 325°F).
7. After the time indicated above has passed, fill the top of the cookie with jam and continue baking for another quarter hour before serving.

Nutrition

- Carbs: 9.9 g
- Cal: 197 kcal
- Prt:6.1 g
- Fats: 14.8 g

6.52 Pepper Parmesan English Muffin

Time for cook: 7 mins. | **Complexity level:** Easy | **Time for prep.:** 5 mins. | **Portions:** 1

Ingredients

- ½ fiber muffin
- 1 tbsp Asiago cheese
- 1 no-calorie butter spray
- A pinch of black pepper
- 1/2 tbsp Parmesan cheese

Execution

1. Toast your muffin in a 325°F preheated air fryer with olive oil.
2. Cook the butter and cheese for 1 minute.
3. Add some freshly ground black pepper on top.

Nutrition

- Carbs: 16.7 g
- Cal: 221 kcal
- Prt:17 g
- Fats: 11.5 g

6.53 Wiener Schnitzel

Time for cook: 10 mins.   **Complexity level:** Easy   **Time for prep.:** 5 mins.   **Portions:** 1

Ingredients

- 1 lb. veal, scallopini cut
- Nonstick cooking spray
- 1 lemon, sliced
- 1 cup breadcrumbs
- 2 tbsp lemon juice
- 1 tbsp chopped fresh parsley
- Salt and pepper as required
- 1 egg
- ¼ cup all-purpose flour

Execution

1. Prepare a 400°F air fryer.
2. Cover the veal in salt and pepper with lemon juice.
3. Combine the egg and parsley in a bowl. Place the breadcrumbs in a different bowl. Flour should cover half of a flat plate.
4. Each veal cutlet should be dredged in flour, then to the egg-parsley mixture, then breadcrumbs, in that order.
5. Spritz the fryer basket. Spray some oil onto the tops. Place breaded veal cutlets in the basket, being cautious not to overcrowd anything.
6. Cooking for 5 mins. per side. Serve with lemon slices on the side.

Nutrition

- Carbs: 27 g
- Cal: 352 kcal
- Prt:33.7 g
- Fats: 11.2 g

6.54 Orange Mustard Glazed Pork Chops

Time for cook: 30 mins.   **Complexity level:** Easy   **Time for prep.:** 12 mins.   **Portions:** 4

Ingredients

- ½ cup fresh orange juice
- 2 tbsp lime juice
- 2 tbsp orange marmalade
- 1 red onion
- ¼ tsp kosher salt
- 1 tbsp whole-grain mustard
- 2 rosemary sprigs
- 1 tbsp canola oil
- ¼ tsp ground black pepper
- 4 pork loin chops

Execution

1. In a pan, mix the juice, marmalade, then mustard. Boil it for a couple of mins., then reduce the heat to low and cook for an additional 15 mins.
2. Season the chops with salt and pepper. Air-fry for about 5 mins. at 375°F.
3. Cook for an extra 5–7 mins. before adding the rosemary, onion, and juice.
4. Lay the pork on a plate and top it with the sauce and lime juice.

Nutrition

- Carbs: 14.7 g
- Cal: 420 kcal
- Prt:53.6 g
- Fats: 15.3 g

6.55 Pizza Hot Dogs

Time for cook: 5 mins.   **Complexity level:** Easy   **Time for prep.:** 10 mins.   **Portions:** 2

Ingredients

- 2 hot dogs
- 2 hot dog buns
- 2 tsp sliced olives
- 4 pepperoni slices, halved
- ¼ cup Mozzarella cheese
- ½ cup pizza sauce

Execution

1. Air-fry the hot dogs for 3 mins. at 390°F. Slit each hot dog 4 times. Move to a cutting board using tongs.
2. Fill the buns with Mozzarella cheese, hot dogs, and olives.
3. Place half a slice of pepperoni in each hot dog slit. Add a little pizza sauce.
4. Add the hot dogs to the air fryer basket and cook them for another 2 mins. to crisp up the cheese.

Nutrition

- Carbs: 30.1 g
- Cal: 354 kcal
- Prt:12.3 g
- Fats: 20.4 g

6.56 Chinese Pork

Time for cook: 10 mins. | **Complexity level:** Easy | **Time for prep.:** 6 mins. | **Portions:** 12

Ingredients

- 1 1/2 lb boneless pork loin
- 1 tbsp olive oil
- 1/3 cup soy sauce
- ½ tbsp minced garlic
- 1 tbsp sesame oil
- 1/3 cup hoisin sauce
- 2 drops of red natural food coloring
- ¼ cup red dry wine
- ½ tsp Chinese 5-spice
- 1 tbsp sugar

Execution

1. Finely slice pork into 3-inch thin strips, then pack in a large sealable plastic bag.
2. Toss the remaining items with a little bit of stirring action in a clean bowl.
3. Spray some olive oil in an air fryer, then cook it all for 2-3 mins. at 350°F. Place the pork with the marinade in a plastic bag. After closing the bag, put it into the fridge for the night.
4. Include the rest of the marinade. Following 10 mins., remove and serve with rice.

Nutrition

- Carbs: 4.9 g
- Cal: 129 kcal
- Prt:15.5 g
- Fats: 4.5 g

6.57 Cream Chipped Beef Upon Toast

Time for cook: 20 mins. | **Complexity level:** Easy | **Time for prep.:** 12 mins. | **Portions:** 1

Ingredients

- 3 oz roast beef
- Pepper to taste
- 1 tbsp butter stick
- 1/2 tsp garlic
- ½ cup skim milk
- ¼ onion
- Salt to taste
- 1 tbsp baking mix

Execution

1. Use the air fryer to sauté onions. Mix in some cubed roast beef and cook for about 3-4 mins. (400°F).
2. Add butter, pepper, garlic, salt, and baking mix at this point, and thoroughly mix everything.
3. Pour the milk in gradually. The beef should be well covered after stirring.
4. Turn the fryer to low and let it simmer for over 5-10 mins. before taking it out.
5. The gravy will thicken as it sits.

Nutrition

- Carbs: 13.6 g
- Cal: 347 kcal
- Prt:30.8 g
- Fats: 17.4 g

6.58 Crustless Pizza Casserole

Time for cook: 25 mins. | **Complexity level:** Easy | **Time for prep.:** 5 mins. | **Portions:** 1

Ingredients

- 1/4 lb Italian ground meat
- 1/3 cup pizza sauce
- Salt and pepper as required
- ½ cup veggies (zucchini, bell peppers, onion, etc.)
- ¼ cup pizza toppings (cheese, onion, pepperoni, black olives, etc.)
- ¼ garlic clove, minced

Execution

1. Cook the vegetables for 2–3 mins., just until tender. Continue to cook at 375°F for another 1–2 mins. after introducing the garlic, salt, and pepper.
2. Add the ground beef and stir-fry it with the vegetables for approximately 10 mins. Empty any extra liquid.
3. Stir in the sauce, then toss for approximately 5-7 mins., preferably until everything is well combined.
4. Evenly distribute the ingredients in the casserole dish after filling it halfway. Put the cheese on top and the garnishes. Cook for 20 more mins.

Nutrition

- Carbs: 25.9 g
- Cal: 524 kcal
- Prt:44.6 g
- Fats: 27.1 g

6.59 Mexicali Meatloaf

Time for cook: 1 hour   **Complexity level:** Difficult   **Time for prep.:** 17 mins.   **Portions:** 2

Ingredients

- 1/4 lb. ground beef
- 1/4 tbsp Montreal steak seasoning
- ¼ cup salsa
- ¼ pack Sazon Goya seasoning mix
- ¼ lb. ground turkey
- ½ tbsp onion powder
- 1 egg
- 1/2 cup shredded cheese
- ½ tbsp garlic powder

Execution

1. Thoroughly combine and integrate all the items. The mixture should feel somewhat moist to the touch but be readily molded into a ball. Add a little more cheese to the mix to thicken it if it appears to be too liquid.
2. Make a sizable loaf, then bake this for 45–60 mins.

Nutrition

- Carbs: 5.5 g
- Cal: 386 kcal
- Prt:43.5 g
- Fats: 21.4 g

6.60 Pork Barbecue

Time for cook: 25 mins.   **Complexity level:** Easy   **Time for prep.:** 5 mins.   **Portions:** 2

Ingredients

- 1/2 package of ribs
- 1 tsp onion powder
- 2 cups water
- 1 tsp salt
- 1 onion
- ½ cup BBQ sauce
- 1 tsp garlic powder

Execution

1. Spray the air fryer with some cooking oil.
2. Cook the ribs, water, onions, and seasonings in the fryer preheated to 400°F for approximately 30 mins.
3. After removing roughly 85% of the liquid, shred the meat with a fork.
4. Cook for an extra 20 mins. after applying the BBQ sauce.
5. You can serve however you think appropriate.

Nutrition

- Carbs: 15.9 g
- Cal: 253 kcal
- Prt:22.7 g
- Fats: 10.8 g

6.61 Ranch Pork Chops

Time for cook: 10 mins.   **Complexity level:** Easy   **Time for prep.:** 7 mins.   **Portions:** 4

Ingredients

- 4 boneless pork chops
- 2 tsp dry ranch mix (salad dressing)
- Olive oil as per need
- Aluminum foil

Execution

1. After applying frying spray on the basket, prep your air fryer to 390°F.
2. Apply cooking spray to both faces of the pork chops before placing them on a dish. Ranch seasoning mix should be sprinkled over both surfaces and left for 10 mins. to set.
3. If necessary, arrange the chops in groups in the air fryer to prevent congestion.
4. After rotating the chops, continue cooking for an extra 5 mins. Before serving, let it sit on a plate covered in foil for over 5 mins.

Nutrition

- Carbs: 2.4 g
- Cal: 271 kcal
- Prt:18.4 g
- Fats: 20.3 g

6.62 Breaded Pork Chops

Time for cook: 10 mins.   **Complexity level:** Easy   **Time for prep.:** 12 mins.   **Portions:** 4

Ingredients

- 4 boneless pork chops
- Cooking spray
- 1 ½ cup cheese with garlic-flavored croutons
- 2 eggs
- 1 tsp Cajun seasoning

Execution

1. Set the air fryer to 390°F.
2. Sprinkle Cajun seasoning over a dish's pork chops' top and bottom surfaces.
3. Coarsely mince croutons in a food processor before transfer to a shallow dish.
4. Beat the eggs separately. After immersing the pork chops in the leftover egg, let it drip off.
5. Spread crouton breading over the chops and arrange them on a plate. Spray some cooking spray on the chops.
6. Arrange chops within the air fryer's basket sprayed with nonstick spray.
7. Cook for 5 mins. Cook for an extra 5 mins. Keep going with the other chops. Flip the chops over and spritz them with cooking spray once more if you notice any spots of dryness or powder on them.

Nutrition

- Carbs: 9.7 g
- Cal: 357 kcal
- Prt:22.4 g
- Fats: 24.8 g

6.63 Baby Back Barbecue Ribs

Time for cook: 35 mins.   **Complexity level:** Medium   **Time for prep.:** 5 mins.   **Portions:** 4

Ingredients

- 3 lb pork ribs
- ⅓ cup BBQ sauce
- 1 tbsp white sugar
- ½ tsp ground cumin
- 1 tbsp brown sugar
- ¼ tsp Greek seasoning (optional)
- 1 tsp smoked paprika
- ½ tsp granulated onion
- 1 tsp sweet paprika
- 1 tsp granulated garlic
- ½ tsp black pepper

Execution

1. Set your air fryer to 350°F.
2. Cut the ribs into 4 evenly-sized pieces after removing the membrane from the rear.
3. Combine white sugar, brown sugar, smoked paprika, sweet paprika, pepper, cumin, Greek spice, garlic, and onion in a bowl. After coating the ribs with the spice mixture, place them in the fryer basket.
4. Cook the ribs for at least 30 mins. and flip them once after 15 mins. Cover with BBQ sauce, then air fry for an additional 5 mins.

Nutrition

- Carbs: 13.6 g
- Cal: 20 kcal
- Prt:15.2 g
- Fats: 10 g

6.64 Berry Chicken Salad

Time for cook: 10 mins.　　**Complexity level:** Easy　　**Time for prep.:** 5 mins.　　**Portions:** 2

Ingredients

- 1 cup chicken meat
- 1/4 tsp ground black pepper
- 1/4 cup blueberries
- 3 strawberries sliced
- 1/3 cup unflavored Greek yogurt
- 1 dash of garlic salt
- 1 tbsp mayo
- 2 tbsp raspberry vinaigrette

Execution

1. Heat the air fryer to 400°F.
2. Coat your air fryer with olive oil and cook the chicken for a long time. After that, shred your chicken.
3. Whisk together the dressing, Greek yogurt, and mayonnaise in a cup.
4. Place your chicken shreds in a bowl and season them with seasonings. Mix everything thoroughly.
5. Add the yogurt/mayo mixture.
6. Add your berries last.

Nutrition

- Carbs: 9 g
- Cal: 204 kcal
- Prt:23 g
- Fats: 8.3 g

6.65 Spinach Apple Salad

Time for cook: 0 mins.　　**Complexity level:** Easy　　**Time for prep.:** 10 mins.　　**Portions:** 4

Ingredients

- ½ cup glazed/toasted walnuts or glazed/toasted pecans
- 1 apple
- 1 best balsamic dressing
- 3 cups baby spinach leaves
- 1 ripe pear
- 3 cups baby mixed greens

Execution

1. Prepare the glazed pecans or glazed walnuts. Make the remainder of the salad while they are cooking.
2. Slice the pear and apple after coring them.
3. Add the apples, pears, and walnuts to the greens on serving plates. Add the dressing and then plate.

Nutrition

- Carbs: 26.8 g
- Cal: 318 kcal
- Prt:3.7 g
- Fats: 23.9 g

6.66 Alfredo Chicken Roulade

Time for cook: 45 mins. **Complexity level:** Medium **Time for prep.:** 7 mins. **Portions:** 1

Ingredients

- 1 tbsp olive oil
- 2 Laughing Cow cheese wedges
- Salt to taste
- 2 cups baby spinach
- ½ onion

- 2 chicken breasts
- ½ the jar of light Alfredo sauce
- Pepper to taste (also other spices)
- 1 red bell pepper

Execution

1. Heat your air fryer to 400°F.
2. Coat the air fryer with some olive oil, then sauté the spinach, onion, and bell peppers until they are cooked to your preference.
3. Prepare chicken breasts by placing them on the board, cutting them into bite-sized pieces, seasoning both sides with salt and pepper, and topping with Laughing Cow cheese.
4. Add extra veggies on top, then roll your chicken breast into Alfredo sauce. Set a 45-minute timer to start cooking when your chicken is ready.

Nutrition

- Carbs: 25.5 g
- Cal: 858 kcal
- Prt:90.8 g
- Fats: 41.1 g

6.67 Chicken with Mushroom

Time for cook: 15 mins. **Complexity level:** Easy **Time for prep.:** 5 mins. **Portions:** 2

Ingredients

- 4 oz fresh mushrooms
- 1/4 cup water
- Pepper to taste
- ¼ pack of Goya seasoning
- ¼ onion, chopped
- 2 cup chicken breast

- Salt to taste
- ½ tsp garlic powder
- 3 ½ oz mushroom soup cream
- 1/2 cup chicken stock
- ½ tsp onion powder

Execution

1. Heat an air fryer to 380°F.
2. Spray the air fryer; sauté the mushrooms and onion.
3. Add the meat, onion powder, stock, garlic powder, Goya, and water. Set a 15-mins. timer while cooking. Add salt and pepper, and serve warm.

Nutrition

- Carbs: 8.1 g
- Cal: 315 kcal
- Prt:43.1 g
- Fats: 11.7 g

6.68 Chili Hot Dog

Time for cook: 30 mins. **Complexity level:** Easy **Time for prep.:** 5 mins. **Portions:** 1

Ingredients

- 1/2 lb turkey meat
- is 2 tbsp chili powder
- Salt to taste
- ½ can of tomatoes
- 2 tbsp tomato paste

- 2 Italian sausage links
- Pepper to taste
- 1/2 cup water
- ¼ tsp olive oil

Execution

1. Heat an air fryer to 325°F.
2. Coat your air fryer with some olive oil, brown your turkey and sausage, and cook for approximately 15-20 mins.
3. Just when the turkey has finished cooking, add your tomato paste. Mix all of the ingredients indicated above before adding the water, and then stir in the chili powder, salt, and pepper.
4. After draining your tomatoes, place them inside the fryer.
5. After bringing everything to a boil, reduce the heat, and set a timer lasting 5 mins.

Nutrition

- Carbs: 15.5 g
- Cal: 433 kcal
- Prt:57.8 g
- Fats: 16.2 g

6.69 Chicken Thighs

Time for cook: 20 mins.   **Complexity level:** Easy   **Time for prep.:** 11 mins.   **Portions:** 4

Ingredients

- 4 boneless chicken thighs
- ¾ tsp garlic powder
- 2 tsp olive oil
- 1 tsp smoked paprika
- ½ tsp ground black pepper
- ½ tsp salt

Execution

1. Create a mixture of paprika, garlic, pepper, and salt in a dish.
2. Take the chicken thighs you will need to cook and grease them with olive oil.
3. Dip the anointed chicken thighs in the spice mixture created earlier, then you are ready to cook them in the air fryer (20 mins. at 400°F)
4. Your chicken will be ready when its internal temperature reaches 165°F. Use a kitchen thermometer to measure it.

Nutrition

- Carbs: 0.9 g
- Cal: 264 kcal
- Prt:20.2 g
- Fats: 19.4 g

6.70 Dry-Rub Chicken Wings

Time for cook: 35 mins.   **Complexity level:** Easy   **Time for prep.:** 12 mins.   **Portions:** 2

Ingredients

- 1 tbsp dark brown sugar
- ½ tsp ground black pepper
- ½ tbsp kosher salt
- 8 chicken wings
- 1 tbsp sweet paprika
- 1 tsp poultry seasoning
- 1 tsp onion powder
- ½ tsp mustard powder
- 1 tsp garlic powder

Execution

1. Set your air fryer at a temperature of 350°F. Mix the paprika, salt, brown sugar, poultry seasoning, garlic powder, pepper, onion powder, and mustard powder in a bowl. Toss chicken wings in and coat well with spices using your hands.
2. Position the wings in the fryer basket to be propped up at their edges.
3. Pressed against one another and the inside of the basket.
4. Cook the wings for approximately 35 mins. until they are crisp on the outer side and tender on the inside. Serve the wings right after placing them on a plate.

Nutrition

- Carbs: 9.4 g
- Cal: 723 kcal
- Prt:20.2 g
- Fats: 73.2 g

6.71 Sugared Pecans

Time for cook: 12 mins.   **Complexity level:** Easy   **Time for prep.:** 5 mins.   **Portions:** 4

Ingredients

- 2 tbsp salted butter
- ¼ tsp ground cinnamon
- ¼ cup white sugar
- 1 cup pecan halves
- 1 egg white

Execution

1. Set your air fryer to 300°F. Use aluminum foil to line the basket.
2. Melt the butter and add it to the ready-made basket.
3. Separately, combine the cinnamon, egg white, and sugar.
4. Stir the pecans in until they are evenly covered. Spread out in the encased basket.
5. Cook for 5 mins. in the air fryer. Shake the basket while allowing the food to air fry for an extra 5 mins. Once again, shake the basket and air fry for an added 2–4 mins.

Nutrition

- Carbs: 13.2 g
- Cal: 127 kcal
- Prt:1.3 g
- Fats: 2.3 g

6.72 Blackened Chicken Breast

Time for cook: 30 mins.   **Complexity level:** Easy   **Time for prep.:** 12 mins.   **Portions:** 2

Ingredients

- 2 tsp paprika
- 12 oz boneless chicken breast
- 1 tsp cumin
- ½ tsp black pepper
- 1 tsp ground thyme
- 2 tsp vegetable oil
- ½ tsp onion powder
- ½ tsp cayenne pepper
- ¼ tsp salt

Execution

1. Set your air fryer to 360°F for preparation. Combine cayenne pepper, cumin, salt, paprika, black pepper, onion powder, and thyme in a single bowl. Put this spice combination on a flat plate.
2. Ensure that each chicken breast is completely coated with oil. Roll each piece of chicken in the spices mixture, pressing firmly to ensure that the spices stick on both sides. While the air fryer gets warm, let the food rest for 5 mins. to settle.
3. Cook the chicken for around 10 mins. Cook for an extra 10 mins. on a second surface. Place the chicken on a dish before serving and give it time to settle, for about 5 mins.

Nutrition

- Carbs: 3 g
- Cal: 250 kcal
- Prt:36.8 g
- Fats: 9.4

6.73 Acorn Squash Slices

Time for cook: 15 mins.   **Complexity level:** Easy   **Time for prep.:** 17 mins.   **Portions:** 2

Ingredients

- 1/6 cup butter
- ¾ acorn squash
- ¼ cup brown sugar

Execution

1. Prep your air fryer to 350°F. Coat the basket with nonstick frying spray.
2. Cut the squash in half vertically to remove the seeds. Slice each serving into crosswise pieces.
3. Place the squash there in the air fryer basket in one layer; cook it for roughly 5 mins. before flipping it over; cook for an extra 5 mins.
4. Spread the squash with a mix of butter and sugar. Cook for another 3 mins.
5. Remove it from the frying, then serve.

Nutrition

- Carbs: 32.8 g
- Cal: 262 kcal
- Prt:1.3 g
- Fats: 15.5 g

6.74 Crispy Cauliflower Tots

Time for cook: 20 mins.   **Complexity level:** Easy   **Time for prep.:** 16 mins.   **Portions:** 2

Ingredients

- ¼ cup cauliflower florets
- ¼ tsp smoked paprika
- 1/3 cup Cheddar cheese
- Salt and pepper to taste
- 1/4 tbsp onion powder
- 1/4 tsp garlic powder
- ½ egg

Execution

1. Heat the air fryer to 400°F.
2. Mix each spice well.
3. Once they are thoroughly combined, crack in an egg and cheese. Add the florets and use a little scoop to mix well. Place the dish onto an air fryer; cook this for roughly 20 mins., turning halfway through.

Nutrition

- Carbs: 1.7 g
- Cal: 79 kcal
- Prt:5.3 g
- Fats: 5.8 g

6.75 Crispy Eggplant Parmesan

Time for cook: 5 mins.   **Complexity level:** Easy   **Time for prep.:** 5 mins.   **Portions:** 1

Ingredients

- 1 eggplant
- 1 egg
- 1 oz Parmesan cheese
- Salt to taste
- ¼ cup almond flour
- ¼ cup breadcrumbs

Execution

1. Preheat the air fryer to 320°F.
2. Cut the eggplant into slender pieces.
3. Coat slices in flour, dip them in egg and then roll them in the cheese, salt, and breadcrumb combination.
4. Spray your slices sparingly.
5. Layer them together to ensure they are crisp; cook them for approximately 3-4 mins. per surface.

Nutrition

- Carbs: 44.5 g
- Cal: 377 kcal
- Prt:15.3 g
- Fats: 17.3 g

6.76 Herb with Lemon Cauliflower

Time for cook: 10 mins.   **Complexity level:** Easy   **Time for prep.:** 9 mins.   **Portions:** 2

Ingredients

- ½ cauliflower head
- ½ tbsp rosemary
- ¼ tsp salt
- 1 tbsp lemon juice
- 1/8 cup parsley
- ½ tbsp thyme
- 1/8 tsp red pepper flakes
- ½ tsp lemon zest
- 2 tbsp olive oil

Execution

1. Set the air fryer's temperature to 350°F.
2. Combine olive oil and cauliflower in a bowl.
3. Set the fryer basket well with florets in it and set a timer for 8–10 mins., stirring halfway through.
4. Combine the remaining items in a dish with 1 tbsp of olive oil.
5. Combine the herb mixture with the cauliflower florets in a bowl, then sprinkle that on top.

Nutrition

- Carbs: 9.1 g
- Cal: 164 kcal
- Prt:3.1 g
- Fats: 14.4 g

6.77 Pepper Poppers

Time for cook: 15 mins.   **Complexity level:** Easy   **Time for prep.:** 22 mins.   **Portions:** 2

Ingredients

- ¼ package of cream cheese
- 2 bacon strips
- ¼ cup Cheddar cheese
- 1/8 cup breadcrumbs
- 1/16 tsp garlic powder
- 1/16 tsp chili powder
- 1/16 tsp salt
- ¼ cup Monterey Jack cheese
- ¼ lb fresh jalapeños
- 1/16 tsp smoked paprika

Execution

1. Prep the air fryer to 325°F.
2. Mix the bacon, cheeses, and seasonings in a large bowl.
3. Fill the bacon combination into each pepper half (1–1 1/2 tbsp). They should be coated with breadcrumbs.
4. Spray a basket of an air fryer, put the poppers in one layer, and set a timer for over 15-20 mins., stopping it just as the cheese starts to melt.
5. Serve alongside dips or sauces.

Nutrition

- Carbs: 8.9 g
- Cal: 291 kcal
- Prt:13.5 g
- Fats: 22.4 g

6.78 Pumpkin Chili

Time for cook: 40 mins.   **Complexity level:** Medium   **Time for prep.:** 10 mins.   **Portions:** 2

Ingredients

- ½ onion, diced
- 1 tbsp olive oil
- 1/2 tsp cinnamon
- 7 1/2 oz canned pumpkin
- ½ garlic clove
- 6 oz tomato soup
- 1/2 tsp coriander
- 1/2 tbsp chili powder
- 1/2 lb lean ground meat
- 4 oz kidney beans
- 1/2 tsp cumin

Execution

1. Prep the air fryer to 325°F.
2. Toss some olive oil in your air fryer. Set a 10-minute timer so that the ground meat is done cooking.
3. Combine tomato soup, pumpkin, beans, spices, onion, garlic, and coriander.
4. Let it boil. Set a timer for over 30 mins. and lower the heat to a reasonable level to simmer it.

Nutrition

- Carbs: 24.9 g
- Cal: 378 kcal
- Prt:35.7 g
- Fats: 15.8 g

6.79 Smoked Spicy and Roasted Brussels Sprout

Time for cook: 20 mins.   **Complexity level:** Easy   **Time for prep.:** 8 mins.   **Portions:** 2

Ingredients

- 5 Brussels sprouts
- 1/4 tsp pepper
- 1/4 cup olive oil
- 1/4 tsp chipotle powder (optional)

- 1/2 tsp cumin
- 1/2 tsp smoked paprika
- 1/4 tsp salt
- 1/2 garlic clove

Execution

1. Prep the air fryer to 400°F.
2. Your Brussels sprouts should be stem-free. Arrange them inside your air fryer.
3. Add oil, garlic, and any other spices after that. Stir until the sprouts are thoroughly covered.
4. Set a 20-minute timer for cooking; allow it to cool before serving.

Nutrition

- Carbs: 6.6 g
- Cal: 248 kcal
- Prt:2.2 g
- Fats: 25.6 g

6.80 Spinach Balls

Time for cook: 25 mins.   **Complexity level:** Easy   **Time for prep.:** 5 mins.   **Portions:** 2

Ingredients

- 1 cup stuffing mix
- 1/4 cup cheese
- 10 oz frozen spinach
- 1/4 butter stick

- 1/4 cup vegetable stock
- 1 egg
- 1/2 tbsp garlic powder
- 1/2 tbsp onion powder

Execution

1. Add some olive oil to your air fryer and warm it to 400°F. Place everything on the list in a bowl and then whisk to combine. Spray your hands with cooking spray as well as the sheet pan.
2. Create 1-inch spinach balls, then equally distribute them on the baking sheet. Set a timer for 10–40 mins. and cook at 400°F until lightly browned. Serve the food hot.

Nutrition

- Carbs: 21.1 g
- Cal: 296 kcal
- Prt:13 g
- Fats: 19.4 g

6.81 Tilapia Milanese

Time for cook: 10 mins.   **Complexity level:** Easy   **Time for prep.:** 6 mins.   **Portions:** 2

Ingredients

- 2 tilapia fillets
- 2 lemon wedges
- ¼ tsp salt
- ¼ cup all-purpose flour
- Cooking spray

- 1 tbsp lemon-pepper seasoning
- 1 egg
- ½ cup Italian-seasoned breadcrumbs
- 2 tbsp lemon juice

Execution

1. Dry the tilapia fillets by patting them with a paper towel. Coat the fish on both faces with flour.
2. Whisk egg, salt, and lemon juice. Combine lemon-pepper seasoning and breadcrumbs.
3. Spray frying oil on the fish. After coating the fish in flour, dip it into the egg and then in the breadcrumbs. Put pressure on the fish to help the breadcrumbs adhere to it.
4. After bringing the air fryer to 400°F, cook the fillets for approximately 5 mins. After turning the fish, cook for an extra 3 mins. Serve with lemon slices on the side.

Nutrition

- Carbs: 36.6 g
- Cal: 262 kcal
- Prt:19.3 g
- Fats: 4 g

6.82 Air Crisp Tilapia

Time for cook: 10 mins.   **Complexity level:** Easy   **Time for prep.:** 6 mins.   **Portions:** 1

Ingredients

- 1 (4 oz) tilapia filets
- 1/2 tsp corn flour
- 1 tsp extra virgin olive oil
- A pinch of red pepper flakes

- 1 minced garlic clove
- Salt to taste
- Pepper as required
- 1 tbsp curry powder

Execution

1. Marinate the fillets for about 15 mins. in a mixture of all the ingredients.
2. Air-fry fillets for 10 mins. at 210°F in the air fryer.
3. Serve warm.

Nutrition

- Carbs: 5.6 g
- Cal: 216 kcal
- Prt:30.4 g
- Fats: 8.9 g

6.83 Tilapia with Fire-Roasted Tomato Sauce

Time for cook: 30 mins.   **Complexity level:** Easy   **Time for prep.:** 12 mins.   **Portions:** 1

Ingredients

- ¼ diced onion
- 1 frozen tilapia fillet
- 3 asparagus stalks
- 1/4 tsp minced garlic

- 1/4 tbsp olive oil
- 1/4 tbsp Cajun seasoning
- 4 oz canned roasted tomatoes

Execution

1. Air-fry onion, garlic, and asparagus over 400°F.
2. Before adding the frozen tilapia fillets, mix fire-roasted tomatoes, then stir thoroughly. Cooking takes 10 mins.
3. Use Cajun seasoning and cover the pan with foil. Cook the salmon for approximately 25 mins. so that it flakes easily with a fork.

Nutrition

- Carbs: 22.8 g
- Cal: 243 kcal
- Prt:30.2 g
- Fats: 6.7 g

6.84 Breaded Sea Scallops

Time for cook: 5 mins.	Complexity level: Easy	Time for prep.: 12 mins.	Portions: 2

Ingredients

- ¼ cup Buttery crackers, crushed
- 1 tbsp melted butter
- ½ lb Sea scallops
- ¼ tsp Garlic powder
- Cooking spray
- ¼ tsp Seafood seasoning

Execution

1. Toss butter onto the scallops.
2. Sprinkle garlic powder and seasoning before rolling in crushed crackers.
3. Air fried approximately for 2 mins. for each side at 400°F.

Nutrition

⬚ Carbs: 13.9 g	⬚ Cal: 217 kcal	⬚ Prt:20.1 g	⬚ Fats: 8.7 g

6.85 Fake Grits

Time for cook: 15 mins.	Complexity level: Easy	Time for prep.: 12 mins.	Portions: 1

Ingredients

- ¼ cup water
- Salt as required
- ½ cup cauliflower florets
- 1 tsp ground Parmesan cheese
- 1 tbsp cream soup
- Pepper as required
- 1 tbsp milk

Execution

1. Air-fry veggies at 400°F for 10-15 mins.
2. Wash and mash the vegetables. Thoroughly mash cauliflower florets in the mixture. If florets develop, keep mashing.
3. Combine the cream soup, cheese, and milk. Season with salt and pepper. Add additional soup and milk to make thinner "grits."

Nutrition

⬚ Carbs: 22.4 g	⬚ Cal: 290 kcal	⬚ Prt:33.8 g	⬚ Fats: 9.3 g

6.86 Fish Sticks

Time for cook: 10 mins.	Complexity level: Easy	Time for prep.: 12 mins.	Portions: 2

Ingredients

- ½ lb cod fillets
- Cooking spray
- 1 tbsp all-purpose flour
- ¼ tsp black pepper
- ½ egg
- ½ tbsp parsley flakes
- 1 tbsp grated Parmesan cheese
- ¼ cup panko breadcrumbs
- ½ tsp paprika

Execution

1. Use paper towels to dry the fish before chopping it into sticks.
2. In 3 individual bowls, combine the flour, the egg, and the panko with the Parmesan cheese, paprika, parsley, and pepper.
3. Dip the fish stick in the egg, then in the flour, and then into the seasoned panko.
4. Before putting the sticks inside your air fryer's basket, spray them with cooking spray. Cook for 5 mins. on each side in a fryer prep to 400°F.

Nutrition

⬚ Carbs: 16.8 g	⬚ Cal: 328 kcal	⬚ Prt:48.6 g	⬚ Fats: 7.3 g

6.87 Lobster Faux and Mac Cheese

Time for cook: 40 mins. | **Complexity level:** Medium | **Time for prep.:** 12 mins. | **Portions:** 2

Ingredients

- 4 oz lobster meat
- Pepper to taste
- 1 spaghetti squash
- 1 1/2 cups sharp cheese
- 4 pork bacon slices, cooked

- 2 tbsp butter
- Salt to taste
- ½ lemon
- 1 1/2 cup milk
- 2 tbsp low-carb baking mix

Execution

1. Cook lobster over 5–7 mins. at 380°F in your fryer.
2. Cook the squash in there until it is tender.
3. Milk, butter, and baking are brought to a boil. The cheese has now been added; keep heating until completely melted. Add salt and pepper to taste. Once this sauce has been prepared, serve it.
4. Stir in the lobster, then sprinkle the cheese over the top. Set the timer for approximately 30 mins. and bake.

Nutrition

| ⬚ Carbs: 17.7 g | ⬚ Cal: 628 kcal | ⬚ Prt:38.9 g | ⬚ Fats: 45.1 g |

6.88 Spaghetti Squash with Ramen

Time for cook: 30 mins. | **Complexity level:** Medium | **Time for prep.:** 17 mins. | **Portions:** 1

Ingredients

- 1/2 cup cooked spaghetti squash
- 1/2 hard-boiled egg
- 1/2 tsp sesame oil
- 1/2 hot chili pepper
- 1/2 tsp soy sauce
- ½ garlic clove, peeled

- 1/4 tsp ginger, grated
- 1 tbsp green onion, chopped
- 1 cup chicken broth
- 4 shrimp
- 4 mushrooms, sliced

Execution

1. Remove the spaghetti squash's seeds and pulp, then drizzle over sesame oil. Transfer to the air fryer and mix the soy sauce, ginger, garlic, chili, green onion, chicken broth, and sesame oil. Roast for about 20 mins.
2. Cook for 5–10 mins. Add the frozen shrimp to the mix and cook until done. A few mins. before the cooking period is complete, add the mushrooms. Cook one egg lasting 8 mins. to prep a hard-boiled egg in the meantime.

Nutrition

| ⬚ Carbs: 12.1 g | ⬚ Cal: 224 kcal | ⬚ Prt:28.9 g | ⬚ Fats: 6.8 g |

6.89 Thai Tuna Sliders

Time for cook: 15 mins. | **Complexity level:** Easy | **Time for prep.:** 6 mins. | **Portions:** 1

Ingredients

- 1/4 can of tuna
- A pinch of cayenne pepper
- 1 tbsp textured vegetable protein
- A pinch of ground ginger

- ½ egg
- A pinch of chili powder
- 1/2 tsp lime juice

Execution

1. Mix the liquid from the tuna and tuna with the TVP. Mix well, then set away for approximately 2–3 mins. to allow the liquid to permeate the top.
2. Mix the seasonings and lime juice thoroughly before introducing the egg.
3. Shape the tuna mixture into slider-size patties. Combine all ingredients well, then place the patties into the fryer.
4. Prepare an air fryer up to 400°F and cook the patties for 4–5 mins. for each side.
5. Add desired garnishes before serving.

Nutrition

| ⬚ Carbs: 1.2 g | ⬚ Cal: 129 kcal | ⬚ Prt:17.5 g | ⬚ Fats: 5.9 g |

6.90 Tilapia Verde

Time for cook: 15 mins.	Complexity level: Easy	Time for prep.: 5 mins.	Portions: 1

Ingredients

- 2 tbsp water
- Salt as required
- ¼ small onion
- 1/2 tilapia filets
- 1/2 cup baby spinach
- Pepper to taste
- 1/8 yellow squash
- 1/2 tsp minced garlic
- 1/4 cup salsa verde

Execution

1. Steam veggies in a preheated air fryer at 325°F.
2. Season the fish with salsa, salt, and pepper. Cook for 15 mins. Serve after taking out.

Nutrition

⬜ Carbs: 5.7 g	⬜ Cal: 85 kcal	⬜ Prt:12.8 g	⬜ Fats: 1.5 g

6.91 Mustard Crab Cake

Time for cook: 15 mins.	Complexity level: Easy	Time for prep.: 5 mins.	Portions: 2

Ingredients

- 1 cup plain breadcrumbs
- 1/2 cup panko breadcrumbs
- 1 egg
- Cooking spray as needed
- 1 yellow onion, diced
- 1/4 tsp kosher salt
- 2 tbsp light mayonnaise
- 1 oz fresh crab meat
- 1 tsp seafood seasoning
- 1 tbsp mustard
- 1 tsp Worcestershire sauce

Execution

1. Carefully stir the crab meat to a mixture of plain breadcrumb, salt, Worcestershire sauce, mustard, onion, egg, mayonnaise, and seafood spice.
2. Shape the crab mixture into patties and sprinkle over the panko breadcrumbs on both sides.
3. Let the food settle for 15 mins..
4. Fry the patties for 15 mins. at 350°F inside the air fryer.

Nutrition

⬜ Carbs: 69.1 g	⬜ Cal: 456 kcal	⬜ Prt:16.9 g	⬜ Fats: 12.2 g

6.92 Crumbed Fish

Time for cook: 12 mins.	Complexity level: Easy	Time for prep.: 12 mins.	Portions: 4

Ingredients

- 1 cup breadcrumbs
- 1 beaten egg
- 4 flounder fillet
- 1 lemon, sliced
- ¼ cup vegetable oil

Execution

1. Set your air fryer to 350°F.
2. In a bowl, combine breadcrumbs and oil. Stir the ingredients until it's loose and crumbly.
3. Completely and evenly coat the fillets with the beaten egg and the breadcrumbs combination.
4. Gently place these coated fillets in the air fryer. Cook lasted approximately 40 mins. until the fish easily flakes with a fork. Use slices of lemon to garnish.

Nutrition

⬜ Carbs: 20.9 g	⬜ Cal: 396 kcal	⬜ Prt:35.8 g	⬜ Fats: 18.1 g

6.93 Pretzel-Crusted Catfish

Time for cook: 10 mins.	**Complexity level:** Easy	**Time for prep.:** 17 mins.	**Portions:** 4

Ingredients

- 4 (6 oz) catfish fillets
- Lemon slices, optional
- ½ tsp pepper
- 4 cups honey mustard pretzels
- 1/2 cup all-purpose flour
- ½ tsp salt
- Cooking spray
- 1/3 cup Dijon mustard
- 2 tbsp 2% milk
- 2 large eggs

Execution

1. In a dish, mix eggs, mustard, and milk and create a well-mixed mixture.
2. In another dish, place the flour.
3. After seasoning the catfish with salt and pepper, coat each fillet first in the flour, then in the created liquid mixture, and finally, top with pretzels.
4. When all the fillets are ready, you should cook them in the air fryer for 25 mins. at 325°F.
5. Use a basket greased with cooking spray for cooking. When your fish is ready, serve it with lemon.

Nutrition

⬚ Carbs: 61.3 g	⬚ Cal: 550 kcal	⬚ Prt:36.7 g	⬚ Fats: 17.1 g

6.94 Swordfish Kebabs

Time for cook: 10 mins.	**Complexity level:** Easy	**Time for prep.:** 12 mins.	**Portions:** 2

Ingredients

- 1 swordfish steak
- 1 onion
- 1 bell pepper
- 1 lemon
- 1 zucchini
- Salt and pepper to taste

Execution

1. Chop the fish into bite-sized pieces while the wooden skewers are soaked in water for about 10 mins. Finely dice the onion, zucchini, and bell peppers.
2. After skewering all of the contents, season the kebabs with salt and pepper.
3. Set your air fryer up to 375°F and set a 10-minute timer. Finely chop the lemon before going into the frying basket. Place the kebabs over the lemon slices.

Nutrition

⬚ Carbs: 15.6 g	⬚ Cal: 147 kcal	⬚ Prt:16.2 g	⬚ Fats: 3.2 g

6.95 Coconut-Breaded Cod

Time for cook: 10 mins.	**Complexity level:** Easy	**Time for prep.:** 12 mins.	**Portions:** 4

Ingredients

- 6 oz cod fillets
- 3 tbsp heavy cream
- ½ cup Parmigiano-Reggiano Cheese
- ¼ cup + 2 tbsp coconut aminos, divided
- 1 tsp chipotle pepper
- ⅓ cup coconut flakes
- 3 egg yolks
- 1/2 cup garlic breadcrumbs
- 1 tbsp sucralose sweetener
- 2 tsp salt

Execution

1. Marinate cod for 8 hours in 1/4 cup of coconut aminos.
2. Combine breadcrumbs, salt, chipotle pepper, coconut flakes, Parmigiano-Reggiano cheese, and sugar in a food processor; process until a fine powder is formed.
3. Combine the cream, 2 tbsp coconut aminos, and egg yolks in a dish to make the egg wash. To make the egg wash, combine the cream, egg yolks, and coconut aminos in a single dish.
4. Coat the fish fillets in egg wash, then thoroughly dredge them in breadcrumbs.
5. Cook your food in an air fryer at over 360°F for around 7–8 mins.

Nutrition

Carbs: 18. g	Cal: 280 kcal	Prt: 16. g	Fats: 15. g

6.96 Protein Ranch Dip

Time for cook: 0 mins. | **Complexity level:** Easy | **Time for prep.:** 2 mins. | **Portions:** 2

Ingredients

1/8 cup Greek yogurt

1/2 tbsp ranch seasoning

Execution

Mix up some plain Greek yogurt with ranch seasoning. Stir well to mix.

Serve on top of a salad or with raw vegetables.

Nutrition

Carbs: 2 g | Cal: 78 kcal | Prt:2 g | Fats: 0 g

6.97 Pickled Red Onions

Time for cook: 0 mins. | **Complexity level:** Easy | **Time for prep.:** 10 mins. | **Portions:** 4

Ingredients

- 1 red onion
- 1 cup apple cider vinegar
- ¼ tsp black pepper
- 1 bay leaf
- 1 tbsp Truvia/Splenda

- ¼ tsp cumin
- ½ tsp kosher salt
- ½ tsp oregano
- 2 garlic cloves

Execution

1. Put the red onion slices in a big Mason jar.
2. Bring the vinegar, bay leaf, salt, black pepper, cumin, garlic, and oregano to a boil in a small saucepan.
3. Pour the warm vinegar spice mix slowly and gently over the red onion.
4. Allow it cool for approximately 15 mins., then cover it with a lid and secure it tightly. Gently shake the jar to mix the spices, then turn it upside down onto the heatproof surface so it cools entirely.
5. Before using or opening, store in the refrigerator for at least 3 days.

Nutrition

Carbs: 3 g | Cal: 43 kcal | Prt:2 g | Fats: 2g

Comfort Foods

6.98 Pumpkin Custard

Time for cook: 0 mins. | **Complexity level:** Easy | **Time for prep.:** 7 mins. | **Portions:** 1

Ingredients

- 1 can of pumpkin
- Whipped cream (optional)
- 3/4 cup Splenda granulated
- 1 can of Carnation evaporated milk
- 1 tsp cinnamon

- 3 eggs
- ½ tsp ginger
- ½ tsp salt
- ¼ tsp cloves

Execution

1. Combine pumpkin, cloves, Splenda, ginger, cinnamon, and salt in a big container. Stir in the eggs.
2. Stir in the evaporated milk gradually.
3. Pour into a shallow casserole dish.
4. Bake for approximately 30–40 mins. inside a 325°F oven until a knife poked near the core comes out clean.
5. Cool on the wire rack. Serve hot or cold.
6. Add the whipping cream before serving.

Nutrition

Carbs: 4 g | Cal: 15 kcal | Prt:17 g | Fats: 1 g

Bonus: Mindful Eating Skills

Tips for dining out and navigating social situations while on a diet.

Eating out and socializing with friends and family can be challenging while on the Gastric Sleeve Diet. The diet has specific guidelines and restrictions that can make it difficult to find menu options that fit within the diet plan. However, with some planning and straightforward strategies, you can successfully navigate these situations and enjoy meals without compromising your diet.

Mindful eating is a practice that entails paying attention to the present moment while eating without distractions or self-judgment. It involves being conscious of the food you eat, how it tastes, and how it makes you feel. This approach is essential for those on a gastric sleeve diet, as it can help them make more mindful food choices, avoid overeating, and better enjoy their meals. When dining out, mindful eating can be advantageous as it can help individuals make more conscious food choices and avoid overeating.

By following these tips and strategies, you can successfully navigate dining out and social situations while on the Gastric Sleeve diet

Plan ahead: Before heading out to a restaurant or social event, look at the menu online and plan for what you will order; this will help you stay on track with your diet and avoid any last-minute decisions that could lead to overeating.

Communicate your needs: Don't be afraid to speak up and tell your server or host about your dietary restrictions. Many restaurants are happy to accommodate special requests, and it's better to be upfront about your needs than struggle with finding something to eat later.

Don't be afraid to ask for modifications: If something on the menu you would like to order is not quite in line with your diet, don't be scared to ask for changes. For example, if a dish has a sauce you can't have, ask for it on the side or without it.

Be mindful of portion sizes: Even if you're ordering something on your diet plan, be aware of how much you eat. Ask for a to-go box, take some home, or share a dish with a friend.

Stay focused on your goals: Remember why you're on a diet and keep your goals in mind. It's okay to indulge occasionally, but don't let one meal or event derail your progress.

Bring your food: If you're attending a social event where food will be served, and you're not sure what will be available, consider bringing your dish to share. This way, you'll know you have something you can eat, and you'll be able to share your progress with others.

Practice Mindful Eating: When you're eating out, try to be present at the moment and pay attention to your food. Avoid distractions like phones or TV and focus on your food's flavors, textures, and smells.

Be prepared for setbacks: It's normal to slip up and make mistakes, but don't let that discourage you. Get back on track as soon as possible, and don't beat yourself up over it.

Have a support system: Surround yourself with people who support and understand your journey. Share your progress and lean on them for support when things get tough.

Remember that progress is progress: Every step forward, no matter how small, is progress. Be proud of yourself and the progress you've made. Remember that you are in control of your journey.

Remember why you started: When dining out or socializing, it is easy to become discouraged or tempted to stray from the diet. Remembering why you started the Gastric Sleeve Diet and your progress can help you stay motivated and on track.

Dealing with Slip-Ups

If you accidentally eat something that is not on your approved list,

It's important to remember that slip-ups are a normal part of any diet, and the gastric sleeve diet is no exception. The key is not to let one slip-up derail your entire progress.

First, it's essential to understand that slip-ups happen to everyone and are not the end of the world. Instead of beating yourself up, take the opportunity to learn from the experience and make a plan to prevent similar slip-ups in the future.

Be kind to yourself, and don't let one mistake become a self-sabotage pattern

One strategy for getting back on track after a slip-up is to get right back to the approved foods and portion sizes as soon as possible. Don't try to "make up" for the slip-up by skipping a meal or drastically reducing your portions; This can lead to overeating later.

Another strategy for dealing with slip-ups is to refocus on your goals and remind yourself why you started the gastric sleeve diet in the first place. Remind yourself of the benefits you've already seen and hope to see.

Identify the emotions or situations that lead to emotional eating and develop a plan to handle them in the future; this may include finding healthier coping methods, such as exercise or meditation. Addressing any emotional eating triggers that may have led to the slip-up is also essential.

Finally, it's important to remember that slip-ups are not failures; they are simply a part of the process. With the right mindset and strategies, you can overcome any slip-ups and continue progressing on your gastric sleeve diet. Keep moving forward and stay committed to your goals.

Tips for avoiding emotional eating

Find your triggers. Find out what circumstances, emotions, or people cause you to turn to food when upset, and devise a strategy to avoid or deal with those triggers.

Find alternative coping mechanisms: Find constructive ways to deal with your feelings, such as walking, practicing meditation, or conversing with a friend.

Mindfulness: When you are eating, bring your awareness to your thoughts, feelings, and physical sensations, and stop when you feel satisfied.

Maintain a food diary: Keep a food journal in which you record everything you eat, how you feel, and any events or triggers that may have led to you indulging in emotional eating.

Distract yourself: When you feel the urge to eat because of your emotions, it is essential to try to divert your attention by doing something else, such as calling a friend, reading a book, or watching a movie.

Keep "trigger" foods out of the house. If you know that certain foods cause you to overeat when feeling emotional, remove them from the home so you won't be tempted to eat them.

Find healthy alternatives: Look for nutritious alternatives to the comfort foods you typically consume when feeling emotional, such as fruit, yogurt, or nuts, and try those.

Self-compassion means being kind to yourself and keeping in mind that making mistakes is a natural and acceptable part of the process and that you can always begin the following day again.

Reward yourself for your efforts: Reward yourself for your efforts by doing something you enjoy whenever you successfully resist the emotional urge to eat, such as taking a bubble bath, treating yourself to a new book, or going to the movies.

Understanding Hunger and Fullness

One of the most important aspects of mindful eating is understanding the difference between true hunger and emotional hunger. True hunger is a physical sensation characterized by a growling stomach, low energy, and difficulty concentrating. On the other hand, emotional hunger is driven by emotions such as stress, boredom, or sadness and is often accompanied by cravings for specific foods.

Learning to identify genuine hunger and fullness cues is essential to eat mindfully. After gastric sleeve surgery, it's important to listen to your body and eat only when you're hungry and stop when you're satisfied but not complete. It's hard at first, but it gets easier.

To help you distinguish true hunger from emotional hunger, we suggest trying the following:
- Keep a hunger and fullness journal to track your physical sensations before and after meals
- Practice mindful eating techniques, such as savoring and enjoying your food
- Try distracting yourself when you feel a craving and wait for the feeling to pass

Mindful Eating Techniques

Mindful eating is the practice of paying attention to the experience of eating and listening to your body's hunger and fullness cues. It is about enjoying your food, savoring its flavors and textures, and being present at the moment. Mindful eating can help you eat less, lose weight, and improve your overall well-being.

By practicing these techniques, you can develop a healthy relationship with food and overcome the emotional triggers that often lead to overeating.

Eating slowly and savoring each bite allows you to enjoy your food entirely, giving your body time to register fullness. Take small bites and chew each one thoroughly before swallowing. Set a timer for 20 mins. and see how long it takes you to finish your meal by eating slowly.

Avoiding distractions while eating: Distractions such as watching TV or using your phone can prevent you from paying attention to your food and your body's hunger and fullness cues. Try eating in a quiet, peaceful place without screens or devices to avoid distractions.

Paying attention to your food's colors, smells, and flavors: This technique helps engage all your senses and fully appreciate your food. To do this, take a moment to look at your food, smell it, and taste it carefully; this will help you to eat more mindfully and to appreciate the food more.

Checking in with your body's hunger and fullness cues throughout the meal: This technique helps you to pay attention to your body's signals and to stop eating when you are satisfied but not overly full. To do this, check in with yourself before, during, and after the meal. Before the meal, ask yourself if you are starving. During the meal, take small breaks and check in with your body's hunger and fullness cues. After the meal, ask yourself if you are satisfied or could have stopped eating earlier.

It's important to remember that mindful eating is a skill that takes time and practice to develop. Start with one technique at a time and be patient with yourself as you work on developing your mindful eating skills. Remember that it is not about perfection but progress; the most important thing is to be kind to yourself and enjoy the journey.

Distinguishing Hunger from Cravings:

As previously stated, it is critical to distinguish between true hunger and emotional hunger or cravings. Emotions, stress, or memories can all trigger cravings for a specific food or flavor. Identify the feeling or emotion driving the craving to differentiate between hunger and cravings. If it's physical hunger, eat; if it's an emotional craving, distract yourself and wait for the sensation to pass.

Practicing Mindful Eating Techniques: It's time to start practicing mindful eating techniques once you've learned to recognize genuine hunger and fullness cues. Paying attention to your eating experience and listening to your body's hunger and fullness cues is what mindful eating entails. It's about appreciating your food, savoring its flavors and textures, and being in the moment. Some practical exercises for practicing mindful eating include:

Eating with your non-dominant hand: This will help you to slow down and pay attention to your food.

Eating with closed eyes will help you focus on your food's flavors and textures.

Eating with chopsticks: This will help you to eat more slowly and to pay attention to your food.

Eating in silence: This will help you to focus on your food and to pay attention to your body's hunger and fullness cues.

Overcoming Emotional Hunger: If you are often driven to eat by emotions, such as stress, boredom, or sadness, try to find other ways to cope with these emotions. Try engaging in activities you enjoy, such as reading, listening to music, walking, or practicing relaxation techniques such as yoga, meditation, or deep breathing.

It's important to remember that mindful eating is a skill that takes time and practice to develop, so start with one technique at a time and be patient with yourself as you work on developing your mindful eating skills. Remember that it's not about perfection but progress; the most important thing is to be kind to yourself and enjoy the journey.

Tips for Overcoming Plateaus

If you're at a plateau in your weight loss journey and feel like you're not making any progress, try incorporating some of these tips into your routine to help you break through it and continue making progress toward your health and fitness goals:

To prevent your body from becoming accustomed to its workout routine and to prevent boredom from setting in, try out some new exercises, ramp up the difficulty or length of your workouts, or switch up the frequency of your activities.

- **Keep a record of your progress.** Keeping a record of your progress can help you see where you need to make changes and can save you motivated to continue working toward your goals. Keeping a journal, utilizing a tracking app, or employing any other successful strategy for you are all viable options for achieving this goal.

- **Get an adequate amount of sleep.** Sleep is necessary for physical and mental recovery, so shoot for seven to nine hours each night.

- **Take control of your stress.** Finding stress-reduction methods like meditation, deep breathing, or exercise that work for you is crucial to weight loss success.

- **Maintain your water intake.** Since drinking a lot of water throughout the day can help flush out toxins and improve digestion, you should maintain your water intake as much as possible.

- **Analyze your diet.** Analyze your diet to ensure you get enough nutrients and determine areas where your diet could be improved.

- **It would help if you looked for assistance.** A support system, whether it consists of friends, family, or a support group, can assist you in staying on track and overcoming any challenges that stand in your way.

You will be better prepared to overcome plateaus and to keep moving toward your health and fitness goals if you implement these tips into your routine and make them a regular part of it.

8-Week Meal Plan

Phase 1 (Clear Liquid)

Week 1

Day 1
Breakfast: Chicken Backs Broth
Lunch: Lemon Thyme Iced Tea
Dinner: Celery Juice
Day 2
Breakfast: Basic Vegetable Stock
Lunch: Clear Tomato Soup
Dinner: Warm Honey Green Tea
Day 3
Breakfast: Lemon Basil Iced Tea
Lunch: Blackberry Mint Ice Tea
Dinner: Vegan Gelatin
Day 4
Breakfast: Lemon and Pepper Tea
Lunch: Chicken Backs Broth
Dinner: Mint Tea
Day 5
Breakfast: Iced Peach Ginger Tea
Lunch: Anti-Inflammatory Golden Tonic
Dinner: Sugar Free Decaf Fruit Punch
Day 6
Breakfast: Lavender Lemonade
Lunch: Strawberry Peach Jell-O
Dinner: Fresh Fruit Popsicles
Day 7
Breakfast: Coconut Lime Iced Tea
Lunch: Clear Protein Popsicles
Dinner: Minty Watermelon Popsicles

Week 2

Day 1
Breakfast: Chicken Backs Broth
Lunch: Lemon Thyme Iced Tea
Dinner: Celery Juice
Day 2
Breakfast: Basic Vegetable Stock
Lunch: Clear Tomato Soup
Dinner: Warm Honey Green Tea
Day 3
Breakfast: Lemon Basil Iced Tea
Lunch: Blackberry Mint Ice Tea
Dinner: Vegan Gelatin
Day 4
Breakfast: Lemon and Pepper Tea
Lunch: Chicken Backs Broth
Dinner: Mint Tea
Day 5
Breakfast: Iced Peach Ginger Tea
Lunch: Anti-Inflammatory Golden Tonic
Dinner: Sugar Free Decaf Fruit Punch
Day 6
Breakfast: Lavender Lemonade
Lunch: Strawberry Peach Jell-O
Dinner: Fresh Fruit Popsicles
Day 7
Breakfast: Coconut Lime Iced Tea
Lunch: Clear Protein Popsicles
Dinner: Minty Watermelon Popsicles

Phase 2 (Full Liquid Purees)

Week 3

Day 1
Breakfast: Chocolate Coconut Protein Latte
Lunch: Shrimp Scampi Puree
Dinner: Spaghetti Squash Au Gratin
Day 2
Breakfast: Butternut Squash Soup
Lunch: Apple Pie Protein Shake
Dinner: Turkey Tacos with Refried Beans Puree
Day 3
Breakfast: Shamrock Protein Shake
Lunch: Pureed Chicken Salad
Dinner: Pear & Ricotta Puree
Day 4
Breakfast: Chocolate Coconut Protein Latte
Lunch: Shrimp Scampi Puree
Dinner: Spaghetti Squash Au Gratin
Day 5
Breakfast: Black Bean And Lime Puree
Lunch: Roasted Red Pepper & Butter Bean Puree
Dinner: Red Pepper Enchilada Bean Puree

Day 6
Breakfast: Melon Shake
Lunch: Leek & Potato Soup
Dinner: Strawberry Banana Protein Sorbet

Day 7
Breakfast: Mexican Egg Puree
Lunch: Avocado & Edamame Smash
Dinner: Strawberry Banana Protein Sorbet

Week 4

Day 1
Breakfast: Butternut Squash Soup
Lunch: Apple Pie Protein Shake
Dinner: Turkey Tacos with Refried Beans Puree

Day 2
Breakfast: Mexican Egg Puree
Lunch: Avocado & Edamame Smash
Dinner: Strawberry Banana Protein Sorbet

Day 3
Breakfast: Scrambled Eggs With Black Bean Puree
Lunch: Strawberry Cheesecake Shake
Dinner: Tomato Tarragon Soup

Day 4
Breakfast: PB Banana Protein Shake
Lunch: Chicken & Black Bean Mole Puree

Dinner: Pureed Salsa and Beans
Day 5
Breakfast: Milk Shake
Lunch: Chia Avocado Chocolate Mousse
Dinner: Strawberry Chia Protein Smoothie

Day 6
Breakfast: Scrambled Eggs With Black Bean Puree
Lunch: Strawberry Cheesecake Shake
Dinner: Tomato Tarragon Soup

Day 7
Breakfast: Butternut Squash Soup
Lunch: Apple Pie Protein Shake
Dinner: Turkey Tacos with Refried Beans Puree

Phase 3 (Semisolid/Soft foods)

Week 5

Day 1
Breakfast: Autumn Egg White Omelet
Lunch: Lean Turkey Chili
Dinner: Pan Seared Tilapia

Day 2
Breakfast: Deviled Egg & Bacon
Lunch: Crockpot Chicken Curry
Dinner: Pan Fried Trout Fillet

Day 3
Breakfast: Mexican Breakfast Casserole
Lunch: Oven-Baked Salmon
Dinner: Black Bean Burger

Day 4
Breakfast: Italian Poached Eggs

Lunch: Pork Taco Soup
Dinner: Crustless Pizza Casserole

Day 5
Breakfast: Curried Lentil Soup
Lunch: Turkey Kale Meatballs
Dinner: Instant Pot Cauliflower Salad

Day 6
Breakfast: Egg White Veggie Scramble
Lunch: Cream Of Mushroom Chicken Thighs
Dinner: Chicken and Bean Bake

Day 7
Breakfast: Italian Poached Eggs
Lunch: Pork Taco Soup
Dinner: Crustless Pizza Casserole

Week 6

Day 1
Breakfast: Mexican Breakfast Casserole
Lunch: Oven-Baked Salmon
Dinner: Black Bean Burger

Day 2
Breakfast: Egg White Veggie Scramble
Lunch: Vegetarian Chili
Dinner: Spicy Summer Beans & Sausage

Day 3
Breakfast: Meatless Mexican Frittata
Lunch: Greek Turkey Burgers
Dinner: Savory Quinoa Muffins

Day 4
Breakfast: Egg White Veggie Scramble
Lunch: Cream Of Mushroom Chicken Thighs
Dinner: Chicken and Bean Bake

Day 5
Breakfast: Egg White Veggie Scramble
Lunch: Vegetarian Chili
Dinner: Spicy Summer Beans & Sausage

Day 6
Breakfast: Deviled Egg & Bacon
Lunch: Crockpot Chicken Curry
Dinner: Pan Fried Trout Fillet

Day 7
Breakfast: Autumn Egg White Omelet

Lunch: Lean Turkey Chili
Dinner: Pan Seared Tilapia

Phase 4 (Reintroduction of Solid foods)

Week 7

Day 1
Breakfast: Spinach and Mushroom Omelette
Lunch: Dumplings
Dinner: Muffin Pizzas
Day 2
Breakfast: Garlic Cheese Bread
Lunch: Parmesan Ravioli
Dinner: Spinach Apple Salad
Day 3
Breakfast: Corn Pudding
Lunch: Onion Rings and Okra Fries
Dinner: Cream Chipped Beef Upon Toast
Day 4
Breakfast: Toast Sticks
Lunch: Tilapia with Fire-Roasted Sauce of Tomato

Dinner: Italian Sausages, Pepper, and onion
Day 5
Breakfast: Ham plus Cheese Turnovers
Lunch: Ranch Pork Chops
Dinner: Peppermint Mocca Cookies
Day 6
Breakfast: Apple Fritters
Lunch: Hot Dog Chili
Dinner: Fish sticks
Day 7
Breakfast: Sweet Potato Toast containing Spinach &Poached Eggs
Lunch: Spaghetti Squash Ramen with shrimp
Dinner: Berry Chicken Salad

Week 8

Day 1
Breakfast: Pumpkin Custard
Lunch: Smoked Spicy & Roasted Brussels Sprout
Dinner: Salmon Nuggets
Day 2
Breakfast: Chewy Pecan Cookies
Lunch: Mexicali Meatloaf
Dinner: Thai Shrimp Salad
Day 3
Breakfast: Garlic Cheese Bread
Lunch: Chicken with Mushroom
Dinner: Crispy Eggplant Parmesan
Day 4
Breakfast: Angelic Eggs
Lunch: Funnel Cake

Dinner: Roasted Garlic
Day 5
Breakfast: Ham plus Cheese Turnovers
Lunch: Breaded Sea Scallops
Dinner: Berry Chicken Salad
Day 6
Breakfast: Spinach and Mushroom Omelette
Lunch: Alfredo Chicken Roulade
Dinner: Pizza Hot Dogs
Day 7
Breakfast: Pepper Parmesan English muffin
Lunch: Spaghetti Squash with Ramen
Dinner: Baby Back Barbecue

20-Week Meal Plan For Maintenance Phase

Week 1

Day 1
Breakfast: Spinach and Mushroom Omelette
Lunch: Lean Turkey Chili
Dinner: Alfredo Chicken Roulade

Day 2
Breakfast: Egg White Veggie Scramble
Lunch: Chicken Quesadilla Pizza
Dinner: Chicken with Mushroom

Day 3
Breakfast: Angelic Eggs
Lunch: Barbecue Salmon
Dinner: Blackened Chicken Breast

Day 4
Breakfast: Autumn Egg White Omelet
Lunch: Vegetarian Chili
Dinner: Tilapia with Fire-Roasted Tomato Sauce

Day 5
Breakfast: Mexican Breakfast Casserole
Lunch: Pork Taco Soup
Dinner: Chili Hot Dog

Day 6
Breakfast: Italian Poached Eggs
Lunch: Greek Turkey Burgers
Dinner: Crispy Eggplant Parmesan

Day 7
Breakfast: Toast Sticks
Lunch: Oven-Baked Salmon
Dinner: Acorn Squash Slices

Week 2

Day 8
Breakfast: Sunny Side Up Egg
Lunch: Mediterranean Chicken
Dinner: Prawns with Garlic and Lemon

Day 9
reakfast: Egg and Avocado Breakfast Pizza
Lunch: Bean and Cheese Burrito
Dinner: Fish Tacos with Tangy Slaw

Day 10
Breakfast: Protein Pancakes
Lunch: Cajun Shrimp Skillet
Dinner: Low Carb Shepherd's Pie

Day 11
Breakfast: Cheesy Egg White Veggie Breakfast Muffins
Lunch: Smoky Black Bean Soup
Dinner: Cilantro Lime Chicken Skewers

Day 12
Breakfast: Ham and Egg Breakfast Casserole
Lunch: Turkey Sausage and Peppers
Dinner: Baked Cod with Roasted Vegetables

Day 13
Breakfast: Low Carb Waffles
Lunch: Lemon Pepper Chicken Breast
Dinner: Easy Taco Soup

Day 14
Breakfast: Southwestern Breakfast Bowl
Lunch: Grilled Chicken Salad
Dinner: Tuna Patties with Lemon Dill Sauce

Week 3

Day 15
Breakfast: Scrambled Eggs with Cheese and Chives
Lunch: Grilled Salmon with Lemon and Herbs
Dinner: Meatballs in Tomato Sauce

Day 16
Breakfast: High Protein French Toast
Lunch: Tofu Stir-fry with Vegetables
Dinner: Chicken Fajita Skillet

Day 17
Breakfast: Baked Egg in Avocado
Lunch: Cajun Shrimp Skillet
Dinner: Turkey Meatloaf Muffins

Day 18
Breakfast: Protein Pancakes
Lunch: Lemon Pepper Chicken Breast
Dinner: Baked Cod with Roasted Vegetables

Day 19
Breakfast: Egg and Avocado Breakfast Pizza
Lunch: Mediterranean Chicken
Dinner: Prawns with Garlic and Lemon

Day 20
Breakfast: Ham and Egg Breakfast Casserole
Lunch: Smoky Black Bean Soup
Dinner: Low Carb Shepherd's Pie

Day 21
Breakfast: Southwestern Breakfast Bowl
Lunch: Turkey Sausage and Peppers
Dinner: Fish Tacos with Tangy Slaw

Week 4

Day 22
Breakfast: Baked Egg in Avocado
Lunch: Smoky Black Bean Soup
Dinner: Lemon Pepper Chicken Breast
Day 23
Breakfast: Southwestern Breakfast Bowl
Lunch: Cajun Shrimp Skillet
Dinner: Low Carb Shepherd's Pie
Day 24
Breakfast: Protein Pancakes
Lunch: Grilled Salmon with Lemon and Herbs
Dinner: Baked Cod with Roasted Vegetables
Day 25
Breakfast: High Protein French Toast

Lunch: Tofu Stir-fry with Vegetables
Dinner: Chicken Fajita Skillet
Day 26
Breakfast: Scrambled Eggs with Cheese and Chives
Lunch: Turkey Sausage and Peppers
Dinner: Prawns with Garlic and Lemon
Day 27
Breakfast: Ham and Egg Breakfast Casserole
Lunch: Mediterranean Chicken
Dinner: Meatballs in Tomato Sauce
Day 28
Breakfast: Egg and Avocado Breakfast Pizza
Lunch: Turkey Meatloaf Muffins
Dinner: Fish Tacos with Tangy Slaw

Week 5

Day 29
Breakfast: High Protein French Toast
Lunch: Cajun Shrimp Skillet
Dinner: Low Carb Shepherd's Pie
Day 30
Breakfast: Baked Egg in Avocado
Lunch: Smoky Black Bean Soup
Dinner: Lemon Pepper Chicken Breast
Day 31
Breakfast: Protein Pancakes
Lunch: Grilled Salmon with Lemon and Herbs
Dinner: Baked Cod with Roasted Vegetables
Day 32
Breakfast: Scrambled Eggs with Cheese and Chives

Lunch: Mediterranean Chicken
Dinner: Meatballs in Tomato Sauce
Day 33
Breakfast: Ham and Egg Breakfast Casserole
Lunch: Tofu Stir-fry with Vegetables
Dinner: Chicken Fajita Skillet
Day 34
Breakfast: Southwestern Breakfast Bowl
Lunch: Turkey Sausage and Peppers
Dinner: Prawns with Garlic and Lemon
Day 35
Breakfast: Egg and Avocado Breakfast Pizza
Lunch: Turkey Meatloaf Muffins
Dinner: Fish Tacos with Tangy Slaw

Week 6

Day 36
Breakfast: Protein Pancakes
Lunch: Tofu Stir-fry with Vegetables
Dinner: Cajun Shrimp Skillet
Day 37
Breakfast: High Protein French Toast
Lunch: Smoky Black Bean Soup
Dinner: Lemon Pepper Chicken Breast
Day 38
Breakfast: Baked Egg in Avocado
Lunch: Grilled Salmon with Lemon and Herbs
Dinner: Meatballs in Tomato Sauce
Day 39
Breakfast: Scrambled Eggs with Cheese and Chives

Lunch: Turkey Meatloaf Muffins
Dinner: Baked Cod with Roasted Vegetables
Day 40
Breakfast: Ham and Egg Breakfast Casserole
Lunch: Turkey Sausage and Peppers
Dinner: Chicken Fajita Skillet
Day 41
Breakfast: Southwestern Breakfast Bowl
Lunch: Mediterranean Chicken
Dinner: Prawns with Garlic and Lemon
Day 42
Breakfast: Egg and Avocado Breakfast Pizza
Lunch: Low Carb Shepherd's Pie
Dinner: Fish Tacos with Tangy Slaw

Week 7

Day 43
Breakfast: High Protein French Toast
Lunch: Grilled Salmon with Lemon and Herbs
Dinner: Lemon Pepper Chicken Breast
Day 44
Breakfast: Protein Pancakes
Lunch: Smoky Black Bean Soup
Dinner: Fish Tacos with Tangy Slaw
Day 45
Breakfast: Southwestern Breakfast Bowl
Lunch: Turkey Meatloaf Muffins
Dinner: Cajun Shrimp Skillet
Day 46
Breakfast: Ham and Egg Breakfast Casserole

Lunch: Mediterranean Chicken
Dinner: Baked Cod with Roasted Vegetables
Day 47
Breakfast: Baked Egg in Avocado
Lunch: Low Carb Shepherd's Pie
Dinner: Meatballs in Tomato Sauce
Day 48
Breakfast: Scrambled Eggs with Cheese and Chives
Lunch: Tofu Stir-fry with Vegetables
Dinner: Chicken Fajita Skillet
Day 49
Breakfast: Egg and Avocado Breakfast Pizza
Lunch: Turkey Sausage and Peppers
Dinner: Prawns with Garlic and Lemon

Week 8

Day 50
Breakfast: High Protein French Toast
Lunch: Grilled Salmon with Lemon and Herbs
Dinner: Lemon Pepper Chicken Breast
Day 51
Breakfast: Protein Pancakes
Lunch: Smoky Black Bean Soup
Dinner: Fish Tacos with Tangy Slaw
Day 52
Breakfast: Southwestern Breakfast Bowl
Lunch: Turkey Meatloaf Muffins
Dinner: Cajun Shrimp Skillet
Day 53
Breakfast: Ham and Egg Breakfast Casserole

Lunch: Mediterranean Chicken
Dinner: Baked Cod with Roasted Vegetables
Day 54
Breakfast: Baked Egg in Avocado
Lunch: Low Carb Shepherd's Pie
Dinner: Meatballs in Tomato Sauce
Day 55
Breakfast: Scrambled Eggs with Cheese and Chives
Lunch: Tofu Stir-fry with Vegetables
Dinner: Chicken Fajita Skillet
Day 56
Breakfast: Egg and Avocado Breakfast Pizza
Lunch: Turkey Sausage and Peppers
Dinner: Prawns with Garlic and Lemon

Week 9

Day 57
Breakfast: High Protein French Toast
Lunch: Grilled Salmon with Lemon and Herbs
Dinner: Lemon Pepper Chicken Breast
Day 58
Breakfast: Protein Pancakes
Lunch: Smoky Black Bean Soup
Dinner: Fish Tacos with Tangy Slaw
Day 59
Breakfast: Southwestern Breakfast Bowl
Lunch: Turkey Meatloaf Muffins
Dinner: Cajun Shrimp Skillet
Day 60
Breakfast: Ham and Egg Breakfast Casserole

Lunch: Mediterranean Chicken
Dinner: Baked Cod with Roasted Vegetables
Day 61
Breakfast: Baked Egg in Avocado
Lunch: Low Carb Shepherd's Pie
Dinner: Meatballs in Tomato Sauce
Day 62
Breakfast: Scrambled Eggs with Cheese and Chives
Lunch: Tofu Stir-fry with Vegetables
Dinner: Chicken Fajita Skillet
Day 63
Breakfast: Egg and Avocado Breakfast Pizza
Lunch: Turkey Sausage and Peppers
Dinner: Prawns with Garlic and Lemon

Week 10

Day 64
Breakfast: High Protein French Toast
Lunch: Grilled Salmon with Lemon and Herbs
Dinner: Lemon Pepper Chicken Breast

Day 65
Breakfast: Protein Pancakes
Lunch: Smoky Black Bean Soup
Dinner: Fish Tacos with Tangy Slaw

Day 66
Breakfast: Southwestern Breakfast Bowl
Lunch: Turkey Meatloaf Muffins
Dinner: Cajun Shrimp Skillet

Day 67
Breakfast: Ham and Egg Breakfast Casserole
Lunch: Mediterranean Chicken
Dinner: Baked Cod with Roasted Vegetables

Day 68
Breakfast: Baked Egg in Avocado
Lunch: Low Carb Shepherd's Pie
Dinner: Meatballs in Tomato Sauce

Day 69
Breakfast: Scrambled Eggs with Cheese and Chives
Lunch: Tofu Stir-fry with Vegetables
Dinner: Chicken Fajita Skillet

Day 70
Breakfast: Egg and Avocado Breakfast Pizza
Lunch: Turkey Sausage and Peppers
Dinner: Prawns with Garlic and Lemon

Week 11

Day 71
Breakfast: High Protein French Toast
Lunch: Grilled Salmon with Lemon and Herbs
Dinner: Lemon Pepper Chicken Breast

Day 72
Breakfast: Protein Pancakes
Lunch: Smoky Black Bean Soup
Dinner: Fish Tacos with Tangy Slaw

Day 73
Breakfast: Southwestern Breakfast Bowl
Lunch: Turkey Meatloaf Muffins
Dinner: Cajun Shrimp Skillet

Day 74
Breakfast: Ham and Egg Breakfast Casserole
Lunch: Mediterranean Chicken
Dinner: Baked Cod with Roasted Vegetables

Day 75
Breakfast: Baked Egg in Avocado
Lunch: Low Carb Shepherd's Pie
Dinner: Meatballs in Tomato Sauce

Day 76
Breakfast: Scrambled Eggs with Cheese and Chives
Lunch: Tofu Stir-fry with Vegetables
Dinner: Chicken Fajita Skillet

Day 77
Breakfast: Egg and Avocado Breakfast Pizza
Lunch: Turkey Sausage and Peppers
Dinner: Prawns with Garlic and Lemon

Week 12

Day 78
Breakfast: Greek Yogurt Parfait
Lunch: Chicken and Bean Bake
Dinner: Lemon Rosemary Chicken

Day 79
Breakfast: Scrambled Eggs with Black Bean Puree
Lunch: Turkey Kale Meatballs
Dinner: Cream of Mushroom Chicken Thighs

Day 80
Breakfast: Strawberry Cheesecake Shake
Lunch: Mexican Egg Puree
Dinner: Lemon Pepper Shrimp

Day 81
Breakfast: Creamy Coconut Chia Pudding
Lunch: Vegetarian Chili
Dinner: Egg White Veggie Scramble

Day 82
Breakfast: Spinach and Mushroom Omelette
Lunch: Spicy Summer Beans & Sausage
Dinner: Lemon vinaigrette dressing

Day 83
Breakfast: Apple Fritters
Lunch: Pan Fried Trout Fillet
Dinner: Chicken Thighs

Day 84
Breakfast: Angelic Eggs
Lunch: Hummus Chicken Salad
Dinner: Lemon Pepper Chicken Breast

Week 13

Day 85
Breakfast: Berry Chicken Salad
Lunch: Spinach Apple Salad
Dinner: Crustless Pizza Casserole
Day 86
Breakfast: Acorn Squash Slices
Lunch: Crispy Cauliflower Tots
Dinner: Black Bean Burger
Day 87
Breakfast: Tilapia Milanese
Lunch: Fish Sticks
Dinner: Coconut-Breaded Cod
Day 88
Breakfast: Protein Pancakes

Lunch: Smoky Black Bean Soup
Dinner: Meatballs in Tomato Sauce
Day 89
Breakfast: Ham and Egg Breakfast Casserole
Lunch: Mediterranean Chicken
Dinner: Cajun Shrimp Skillet
Day 90
Breakfast: Baked Egg in Avocado
Lunch: Low Carb Shepherd's Pie
Dinner: Grilled Salmon with Lemon and Herbs
Day 91
Breakfast: Greek Yogurt Parfait
Lunch: Tofu Stir-fry with Vegetables
Dinner: Lemon Rosemary Chicken

Week 14

Day 92
Breakfast: Scrambled Eggs with Cheese and Chives
Lunch: Turkey Sausage and Peppers
Dinner: Lemon Pepper Chicken Breast
Day 93
Breakfast: Strawberry Cheesecake Shake
Lunch: Mexican Egg Puree
Dinner: Lemon vinaigrette dressing
Day 94
Breakfast: Creamy Coconut Chia Pudding
Lunch: Vegetarian Chili
Dinner: Egg White Veggie Scramble
Day 95
Breakfast: Spinach and Mushroom Omelette

Lunch: Spicy Summer Beans & Sausage
Dinner: Lemon Rosemary Chicken
Day 96
Breakfast: Angelic Eggs
Lunch: Hummus Chicken Salad
Dinner: Lemon Pepper Shrimp
Day 97
Breakfast: Berry Chicken Salad
Lunch: Spinach Apple Salad
Dinner: Crustless Pizza Casserole
Day 98
Breakfast: Acorn Squash Slices
Lunch: Crispy Cauliflower Tots
Dinner: Black Bean Burger

Week 15

Day 99
Breakfast: Greek Yogurt Parfait
Lunch: Chicken and Bean Bake
Dinner: Lemon Rosemary Chicken
Day 100
Breakfast: Scrambled Eggs with Black Bean Puree
Lunch: Turkey Kale Meatballs
Dinner: Cream of Mushroom Chicken Thighs
Day 101
Breakfast: Strawberry Cheesecake Shake
Lunch: Mexican Egg Puree
Dinner: Lemon Pepper Shrimp
Day 102
Breakfast: Creamy Coconut Chia Pudding

Lunch: Vegetarian Chili
Dinner: Egg White Veggie Scramble
Day 103
Breakfast: Spinach and Mushroom Omelette
Lunch: Spicy Summer Beans & Sausage
Dinner: Lemon vinaigrette dressing
Day 104
Breakfast: Angelic Eggs
Lunch: Hummus Chicken Salad
Dinner: Lemon Pepper Chicken Breast
Day 105
Breakfast: Berry Chicken Salad
Lunch: Spinach Apple Salad
Dinner: Crustless Pizza Casserole

Week 16

Day 106
Breakfast: Acorn Squash Slices
Lunch: Crispy Cauliflower Tots
Dinner: Black Bean Burger
Day 107
Breakfast: Tilapia Milanese
Lunch: Fish Sticks
Dinner: Coconut-Breaded Cod
Day 108
Breakfast: Protein Pancakes
Lunch: Smoky Black Bean Soup
Dinner: Meatballs in Tomato Sauce
Day 109
Breakfast: Ham and Egg Breakfast Casserole

Lunch: Mediterranean Chicken
Dinner: Cajun Shrimp Skillet
Day 110
Breakfast: Baked Egg in Avocado
Lunch: Low Carb Shepherd's Pie
Dinner: Grilled Salmon with Lemon and Herbs
Day 111
Breakfast: Greek Yogurt Parfait
Lunch: Tofu Stir-fry with Vegetables
Dinner: Lemon Rosemary Chicken
Day 112
Breakfast: Strawberry Cheesecake Shake
Lunch: Mexican Egg Puree
Dinner: Lemon vinaigrette dressing

Week 17

Day 113
Breakfast: Creamy Coconut Chia Pudding
Lunch: Vegetarian Chili
Dinner: Egg White Veggie Scramble
Day 114
Breakfast: Spinach and Mushroom Omelette
Lunch: Spicy Summer Beans & Sausage
Dinner: Lemon vinaigrette dressing
Day 115
Breakfast: Angelic Eggs
Lunch: Hummus Chicken Salad
Dinner: Lemon Pepper Chicken Breast
Day 116
Breakfast: Berry Chicken Salad

Lunch: Spinach Apple Salad
Dinner: Crustless Pizza Casserole
Day 117
Breakfast: Acorn Squash Slices
Lunch: Crispy Cauliflower Tots
Dinner: Black Bean Burger
Day 118
Breakfast: Tilapia Milanese
Lunch: Fish Sticks
Dinner: Coconut-Breaded Cod
Day 119
Breakfast: Protein Pancakes
Lunch: Smoky Black Bean Soup
Dinner: Meatballs in Tomato Sauce

Week 18

Day 120
Breakfast: Baked Egg in Avocado
Lunch: Low Carb Shepherd's Pie
Dinner: Grilled Salmon with Lemon and Herbs
Day 121
Breakfast: Greek Yogurt Parfait
Lunch: Tofu Stir-fry with Vegetables
Dinner: Lemon Rosemary Chicken
Day 122
Breakfast: Strawberry Cheesecake Shake
Lunch: Mexican Egg Puree
Dinner: Lemon vinaigrette dressing
Day 123
Breakfast: Creamy Coconut Chia Pudding

Lunch: Vegetarian Chili
Dinner: Egg White Veggie Scramble
Day 124
Breakfast: Spinach and Mushroom Omelette
Lunch: Spicy Summer Beans & Sausage
Dinner: Lemon vinaigrette dressing
Day 125
Breakfast: Angelic Eggs
Lunch: Hummus Chicken Salad
Dinner: Lemon Pepper Chicken Breast
Day 126
Breakfast: Berry Chicken Salad
Lunch: Spinach Apple Salad
Dinner: Crustless Pizza Casserole

Week 19

Day 127
Breakfast: Acorn Squash Slices
Lunch: Crispy Cauliflower Tots
Dinner: Black Bean Burger
Day 128
Breakfast: Tilapia Milanese
Lunch: Fish Sticks
Dinner: Coconut-Breaded Cod
Day 129
Breakfast: Protein Pancakes
Lunch: Smoky Black Bean Soup
Dinner: Meatballs in Tomato Sauce
Day 130
Breakfast: Baked Egg in Avocado
Lunch: Low Carb Shepherd's Pie
Dinner: Grilled Salmon with Lemon and Herbs
Day 131
Breakfast: Greek Yogurt Parfait
Lunch: Tofu Stir-fry with Vegetables
Dinner: Lemon Rosemary Chicken
Day 132
Breakfast: Strawberry Cheesecake Shake
Lunch: Mexican Egg Puree
Dinner: Lemon vinaigrette dressing
Day 133
Breakfast: Creamy Coconut Chia Pudding
Lunch: Vegetarian Chili
Dinner: Egg White Veggie Scramble

Week 20

Day 134
Breakfast: Spinach and Mushroom Omelette
Lunch: Spicy Summer Beans & Sausage
Dinner: Lemon vinaigrette dressing
Day 135
Breakfast: Angelic Eggs
Lunch: Hummus Chicken Salad
Dinner: Lemon Pepper Chicken Breast
Day 136
Breakfast: Berry Chicken Salad
Lunch: Spinach Apple Salad
Dinner: Crustless Pizza Casserole
Day 137
Breakfast: Acorn Squash Slices
Lunch: Crispy Cauliflower Tots
Dinner: Black Bean Burger
Day 138
Breakfast: Tilapia Milanese
Lunch: Fish Sticks
Dinner: Coconut-Breaded Cod
Day 139
Breakfast: Protein Pancakes
Lunch: Smoky Black Bean Soup
Dinner: Meatballs in Tomato Sauce
Day 140
Breakfast: Baked Egg in Avocado
Lunch: Low Carb Shepherd's Pie
Dinner: Grilled Salmon with Lemon and Herbs

Index Of Recipes

If the Gastric Sleeve Bariatric Cookbook has served you well in your gastronomic journey post-gastric sleeve surgery, it would mean a lot to me if you could take a moment to share your thoughts in a review on Amazon. Your feedback can significantly assist others who are on the same path to healthier living.

With heartfelt appreciation,
Raven Foster

Printed in Great Britain
by Amazon

47952746R00071